Do Not QD 182 S2235 78896

INTERNAL BANK AUDITING

Internal Bank Auditing

ESTHER M. SHONT

Vice President
Bankers Trust Company

A WILEY-INTERSCIENCE PUBLICATION

JOHN WILEY & SONS
New York · Chichester · Brisbane · Toronto · Singapore

Library of Congress Cataloging in Publication Data:

Shont, Esther M.
  Internal bank auditing.

  Includes index.
  1. Bank examination.   2. Bank examination—
United States.   I. Title.

HG1707.5.S53   657'.458'024332   82-2851
ISBN 0-471-08918-4   AACR2

Printed in the United States of America

10 9 8 7 6 5 4 3 2 1

To my mother
for her support and encouragement.

Preface

Textbooks on internal bank auditing and bank examinations are not too difficult to find. Most of them, however, are focused on the experienced, professional internal auditor and outside examiner and too often are primarily checklists, auditing questionnaires, or "how to" manuals covering specific functions. Few of them treat in depth, if at all, the philosophy, techniques, objectives, and standards of internal auditing. Either there is no awareness of the large, interested audience outside of the purely professional fraternity of bank auditors and bank examiners or these matters are not considered important enough to be addressed. This audience includes bank employees who are not directly involved in auditing but have a need to know and understand auditing, such as supervisory and operating personnel and even bank management, and people in industry and finance, lawyers, certified public accountants, the general public, and those who must deal with internal auditors, regulatory examiners, and certified public accountants. All of them ought to understand the purpose and objectives of internal auditors and how they differ from those of outside examiners, and in particular bank employees and officers who must cooperate and communicate with regulatory examiners and certified public accountants.

Considering the broad make-up of this audience, one cannot help being struck by the wide differences that must exist in motivation, understanding, educational backgrounds, and experience. The influx of large numbers of foreign banks has further complicated the situation with problems of language and foreign banking practices. Communicating with such an audience demands an approach very different from that employed in the materials on bank auditing currently available.

Successful, experienced bankers who are strong generalists—and today not many bankers are strong generalists—know that for the most part the subject matter of banking is not to be found in texts, but in the heads of experienced bankers. Yet most of the texts available on internal bank auditing or bank examinations assume that the reader is familiar with banking functions, has a good knowledge of bank accounting or is a CPA, is aware of the liabilities inherent in banking functions, and, further, understands the meaning and significance of controls, the various systems of controls, and the critical need for these controls.

Such assumptions have no basis in fact even where most bank employees and managers are concerned. These employees and managers represent a broad cross section of the commercial and savings bank industries and come from all areas of operations, accounting, lending, trust, administration, and wholesale and retail banking. In most instances, they are familiar only with the functions in which they are involved and unfortunately their know-how is in too many cases confined to a specific segment of those functions. They operate the engine rooms of the industry without having the opportunity to study or even view the total structure. Because of the unavoidable fragmentation of modern banking, they are at a tremendous disadvantage and the industry suffers as a consequence. Communicating with them should enjoy a high priority if auditing is to command the respect and cooperation it needs.

Top management today is not much better off, except in rare instances, and it carries the additional burden of responsibility for high-level decision making, accountability for those decisions, and personal liability in the event of substantial loss. Those not yet involved in the industry, that is, students of money and banking at the undergraduate or even graduate level, are still further removed from the basic realities. Professional people such as lawyers and certified public accountants are many times surprisingly uninformed and require considerable briefing.

The importance of internal bank auditing has been steadily growing since 1960. Legislatures, regulatory authorities, and the general public have been questioning the motives, policies, and protective practices of banking with a more than critical eye. Insurance carriers, who could never be characterized as "ready believers," are more challenging than ever. What are the events and conditions that have contributed to these attitudes?

During these years, there has been a rather alarming number of losses and bank failures across the country and abroad, including the failure of at least one large commercial bank in New York City and the near failure of a Philadelphia bank that is the largest and oldest in the state of Pennsylvania. There has always been the fear of the "domino effect" when a large bank fails, although bank regulatory agencies and other banks employ many ways to minimize this effect. It is to be hoped there will be no repetition of the events of the early 1930s.

The accelerating role of automation brings with it many security and operating problems for which reassuring solutions have not yet been found. Unfortunately or fortunately, depending on where you sit, there are many new and startling developments in automation waiting in the wings, and it is almost certain that the present fierce competition in the banking industry will impel banks to take advantage of them.

Competition has motivated banks to offer many new and controversial services that formerly were not considered to be within the province of the industry. Banks have been aggressively challenged by both nonbank competitors, chiefly the securities and investment banking industry, and the regulatory agencies on the legality and propriety of their invasion of these fields. The hostility persists, flaring up into open warfare from time to time.

The increasing incidence of white-collar crime against banks both from within and without as well as crimes of violence are a constant threat to banking's image and credibility. White-collar crime has been aided by automation and stimulated by serious economic and social problems, although it should be stressed that banking is not the only industry that suffers because of inflation and social unrest.

One of the most serious problems, if not the most serious facing banks today is the steady erosion of the supply of basic banking know-how that has been going on since World War II. Before the war began, banking had a captive supply of experienced, dedicated employees who had been in banking since the Great Depression, but these employees have gradually been retiring or resigning to go to better paying jobs. The war, of course, helped to deplete this reservoir of knowledge and experience, but since the end of the war, there have been other forces that are very difficult to combat: the impatience and rising expectations of a new breed of employee who refuses to wait it out until he or she is trained and can prove his or her worth, the fierce competition among banks for relatively experienced people at both the executive and lower levels, and the declining educational standards of the public school systems, which produce graduates who are difficult for industry to train; all of these forces are aggravating the problem. The banking industry itself is making things worse by not conserving its dwindling supply of productive, experienced people and putting them to profitable use, by employing nonbanking people to establish and conduct in-house training programs, and by not listening.

Finally, directors of banks have been made painfully aware of their individual personal liability to customers, stockholders, and the public for loss resulting from negligence, fraud, conflicts of interest, self-dealing, and a myriad of other questionable practices. Their increased interest in internal auditing is not to be wondered at. To whom should they turn for objective, informed appraisals of their banks' systems of accounting, operations, and control? A knowledgeable and competent internal auditing staff led by a strong, respected auditor can be of invaluable assistance to management.

The overriding purpose of this book is to bring to the large, diversified audience of interested readers a clearly defined picture of bank management's need for high-quality internal auditing, and to explain what internal auditing is all about, its purpose, its techniques, and its approach to analyzing and evaluating the critical problems of operating efficiency and safety. A second, but just as important purpose is to give the reader a broad picture of the complex and diversified banking functions that auditors must understand before their objectives can be achieved.

Although this book will concentrate on internal bank auditing, the objectives, philosophy, techniques, and standards discussed are applicable to other industries as well.

ESTHER M. SHONT

New York, New York
February 1982

Contents

1

The Nature of
Internal Bank
Auditing

THE MEANING OF AUDIT, AUDITING, AND AUDITOR

What do the words "audit" and "auditor" mean? What does internal bank auditing mean? What does an internal bank auditor do that differs from what an outside bank auditor does? What is the essential difference between an internal bank auditor and an outside auditor? Who are the outside bank auditors? These and many other questions may very well be puzzling people who have not had an opportunity to get acquainted with this isolated world, but these words are not foreign to the general business reader, who certainly must have some idea of what they mean. Yet it is probable that few general business readers understand their significance in the purely professional sense.

The words "audit" and "auditor" are closely related to words with which most people are familiar even if they are not involved in business and finance. Everyone knows what an auditorium is and almost everyone has been part of an audience at one time or another. As part of an audience, one might go to an auditorium to listen to someone speak or sing or perhaps to watch a presentation. Of course being part of a television audience does not mean that one must go to an auditorium; one may watch and listen at home.

An auditor is defined in Webster's Dictionary as, first, "one that hears or listens," second, "one authorized to examine and verify accounts," third, "one that audits a course of study," and fourth, "one that hears (as a court case) in the capacity of a judge." The word "audit" is derived from the Latin "auditus," the act of hearing, and is further defined as "a formal or official examination and verification of an account book and a methodical examination of books of account by auditors." Although the auditor referred to in these definitions is not strictly speaking the internal auditor with whom this book is concerned, the definitions are nevertheless of great interest with respect to the basic or literal meaning of the words "audit" and "auditor."

If the so-called person in the street or, for that matter, almost anyone in the world of business and finance not directly involved in the auditing profession were asked to pick one of the foregoing dictionary definitions that best describes the internal bank auditor's job, chances are that "one authorized to examine and verify accounts" would be selected. Although this definition would more or less describe the chief occupation of the internal bank auditor many years ago, it is really what the public still believes the internal bank auditor does exclusively today.

On the other hand, if a knowledgeable member of the profession were asked to make the selection, he or she would probably choose all four definitions and might very well explain the selection as follows:

1 "One that hears or listens" applies to both the internal and the outside auditor because this is one technique they both use to gather valuable information. They ask questions and they discuss problems and situations with those who implement the many accounting and operating procedures.

2 "One authorized to examine and verify accounts" obviously applies because it always has been and continues to be an important auditing technique, particularly in periodic complete examinations of a department or division. It is also used on a test basis during interim audits to determine with a reasonable degree of assurance that the bank's asset and liability accounts, its income and expense accounts, and miscellaneous accounts are complete and accurate.

3 "One that audits a course of study" would also be applicable if the words "functions, services, systems, and procedures" were substituted for "course of study," because an auditor must be exceptionally knowledgeable in the subject matter of banking and have detailed understanding of both the operating and administrative sys-

tems employed to carry out the many banking functions. Thus the auditor "audits" or studies the functions and operations to learn and later to stay current on new developments.

4   "One that hears (as a court case) in the capacity of a judge" has special significance to the auditor of today. Modern auditing philosophy and principles require that the auditor, both internal and outside, review, analyze, and weigh the facts (hear evidence), render an opinion (make a judgment), and recommend corrective action where it is necessary (pass sentence).

It is interesting to note that the definition of internal auditing developed and published by the Institute of Internal Auditors and adopted by the auditing profession incorporates to a certain degree some of the basic elements of the Webster four-part definition of an auditor. Their definition, which is really more of a statement of principle, is as follows:

> Internal auditing is an independent appraisal activity within an organization for the review of accounting, financial and other operations as a basis for service to management. It is a managerial control which functions by measuring and evaluating other controls.

There are some new words in this definition that will be examined and explained; not the least of these is the word "controls," which is the topic of the second chapter. The words of immediate significance are "independent appraisal activity," which in retrospect and in light of auditing's history set forth a new and radical concept of the auditing function and the role of the auditor, one from which there seems to be no turning back. These words, "independent appraisal activity," strange as it may seem, are analogous to part four of the Webster definition, "one that hears (in a court case) in the capacity of a judge." Judges perform an appraisal activity throughout a hearing or trial, with or without a jury. The ultimate expression of this appraisal activity, aside from the pronouncement of sentence, is found in the judicial opinions rendered in all the various courts of appeal up to the Supreme Court of the United States.

This definition of internal auditing is very broad and all encompassing and when analyzed, very formidable in its implications and ramifications. It was developed and promulgated by the Institute of Internal Auditors in 1957, when internal bank auditing was beginning to branch out and grow, painfully slowly and most reluctantly and, unfortunately, in not too organized a fashion. Most internal bank auditors were trying very hard to navigate in two worlds: the old one, which they knew and in which they felt comfortable but which they were being forced to leave by an irresistible tide of new forces, and the new one, which they did not fully understand but with which they had to learn to cope to survive.

INTERNAL BANK AUDITING AND THE BANKING ENVIRONMENT BEFORE WORLD WAR II

To fully appreciate the internal bank auditor's dilemma and the enormity of the task before him and even more important, to understand what internal bank auditing means to the profession today, it is necessary to go back in time and take a good look at internal bank auditing as it was some fifty years ago. It is also important to realize that very little change occurred right up to World War II. The tempo of change in banking was as it always had been, slow. Bankers were conservative as always, not openly competitive, and not that concerned, if at all, with the marketability and performance of a bank's stock. It is a very different story today. The bottom line controls everything bankers do. It is promoting cut-throat competition and prompting managers and account officers to think only in terms of short-range goals. This is destructive to the long-term performance of any organization and particularly an industry as sensitive as banking.

At that time, not every bank had an auditor, and even in some of those banks that did, the auditor was, unfortunately, regarded as a necessary evil. This is still true in some banks even today, but with a difference. The auditor may still be just someone to be tolerated, but he has more clout because both the regulatory agencies and the public are on his side. He did not normally occupy a position of high rank and more often than not reported either to the comptroller or, even worse, to an officer in operations. He was on shaky ground and had no independence. Perhaps with the exception of certain very large, prestigious banks, the auditor was definitely "personna non grata," both with management and the general staff. He was told what to do. He had very little, if any, say in the matter and what was even more defeating, probably had very little to contribute in the way of new and constructive ideas. He was not encouraged to think in terms of critiquing audit coverage, operating systems, or procedures or of suggesting improvements. His horizons were very limited, and if he inwardly rebelled, he rarely if ever would have dared to voice his discontent or disagreement. He was subservient, had no independence, and his position in all probability was not provided for in the bylaws of the bank. Those he audited hated and feared him because they realized that if the auditor were to survive, he had to find their mistakes and turn them in. Many held him in contempt. He was considered to be an informer, a policeman, and definitely not one of them.

The position of most auditors in those days was comparable to that of a chief clerk (no longer in existence) who was usually a senior employee with an overall knowledge of the operations of his division or department. Indeed, on the positive side, the auditor usually had a fine understanding of bank accounting and a detailed knowledge of all banking functions (except fiduciary functions) and operations, all acquired over many long and wearisome years. Because of the wall that has always separated the fiduciary functions from commercial banking and because of the aloofness of the fiduciary personnel, auditors normally did not try to learn the trust business and confined their audits to counting securities in the vault, verifying income received and distributed, and checking, albeit in a shallow fashion, the cash and securities statements mailed out to trust customers.

Personal career progress was agonizingly slow throughout the banking industry and the many years of apprenticeship were stifling and disheartening. Almost no one ever dreamed of protesting, not only because it would have been dangerous, but because these conditons were accepted as a way of life. Bank employee morale was sustained and personal dignity reinforced by the pride instilled in them by public approval of their positions as bank employees. In their local communities, head tellers were often referred to as bankers and enjoyed a great deal of prestige. It must be remembered that in those days head tellers really knew infinitely more about banking in general than tellers do today. In many ways they no doubt deserved the title of "banker." The were given plenty of time to learn.

Salaries were very low, lower than in comparable positions in other industries, but employees were comforted by the belief that their jobs were secure as long as they didn't steal or commit some other crime. That was substantially true, at least after the firings prompted by the Great Depression had come to an end, and banks sought to promote the idea. It is no longer true today and hasn't been for at least the last ten years. However, salaries and benefits are infinitely better, even competitive. There was no realistic salary policy or salary administration. For example, in 1943, when the United States was at war and there was, so to speak, an employees' market, a college graduate (not Ivy League) entering an auditing department of any large New York City bank as a beginner received about thirty dollars a week, whereas a stenographer entering at the same time received about five dollars less. A college degree therefore was worth about five dollars more than a high school diploma.

Employees were almost completely regimented, and to some degree, even in their personal lives. With few exceptions, most female employees were either secretaries or typists, and if they decided to get married and were indiscrete enough to make it known, they were forced to leave their jobs. Married women were not supposed to work because it took jobs away from men. Unmarried men were not discriminated against, but if they didn't get married, the bank was uneasy. At one time, however, a man had to ask permission when he wanted to get married because, as the bank explained, they wanted to make sure he would be able to support a wife and eventually children. So much for unwarranted intrusions into peoples' private lives. That was the way it was.

While these details have nothing to do with auditing per se, they do paint a vivid picture of an environment totally foreign to most people today and give the reader some idea of the rigid, paternalistic, and archaic attitudes of management in the past. Believe it or not, some of these attitudes still operate today, underground. In such an environment it was to be expected that lower-level management would copy or adopt the attitudes of their superiors (protective coloration), and certainly the chief auditor was no exception. If anything, he had a tendency to translate these attitudes into action above and beyond what was originally intended. He assumed the role of policeman, which of course filtered down to the rest of the auditing staff, who in turn tended to act like policemen in their everyday encounters with the operating people they were auditing.

There was very little turnover in those days because jobs were almost nonexistent as a result of the Great Depression. Consequently, the employees of the 1930s stayed put until the beginning of World War II, exerting their conditioning on the new employees coming in to replace the men who were being drafted to serve in the armed forces. People still continued to be reluctant to express an opinion and supervisors and officers were still strict disciplinarians. Conditioning of fear dies hard. Although it was not an environment conducive to truth, innovation, creativity, or progress, it had one thing going for it which the banking industry wishes it had today and which it will never have again: There was a great reservoir of banking know-how being passed on to succeeding generations of bankers. This of course started to disappear after the war ended. Downtrodden bank employees who felt they could afford it left the banks for jobs in industry, which were opening up at a great rate and at much higher salaries. There were fewer and fewer well-trained people to train newcomers, and so started the great erosion of banking's reservoir of knowledge and technical expertise. Banking was slow to recognize what was happening and never realized what it was losing until it was gone.

In those banks where the need for an auditing department was recognized by management, the auditor had a staff. The size of the staff depended of course on many things: the budget, which was always inadequate; the size of the bank; and the ability of the auditor to correctly estimate his requirements and persuade management to accept them, always of course providing that he had the intestinal fortitude to do so. His source of supply at that time was, in too many instances, the cast-offs from other departments. This practice of course accurately reflected the real attitude of management toward the auditing function. It also told the world something about management's lack of understanding of the real purpose and objectives of internal auditing, its basic cynicism, and its inability to effectively diagnose and manage personnel problems. If an individual could not get along with his superior, if the superior simply did not like him, or if he did not perform, the answer was to dump him in the auditing department. Naturally, this practice did not make for great morale, it hampered the development of a knowledgeable and effective staff, and what was more, it stacked, the cards against these people. Their qualifications or lack thereof were never questioned and it is doubtful that much serious thought had ever been given to what an auditor's qualifications should be. The cast-offs were not, of course, necessarily incompetent or unwilling to exert themselves; they were simply lost. It is common knowledge that people are all too often either incorrectly evaluated, or not appraised at all, and that personality conflicts are often resolved by getting rid of the troublesome individual. Personnel management, like auditing, had not come into its own as yet, but the real explanation was that business had become accustomed to a captive working force because there had been severe unemployment for many years.

Educational requirements varied from bank to bank and from region to region, but it is safe to say that as long as the applicants were high school graduates who could read, write, and do simple arithmetic, they were deemed qualified for most operational and administrative jobs. This attitude did not prevail where the prospective candidate was expected to deal with executives of present and future corporations and wealthy individual customers. The bank account officer, or relationship manager as he is now called, was a person of prestige. Account officers were recruited, as they still are, from the best universities, or at least from the most prestigious universities, such as Harvard, Yale, Princeton, Dartmouth, and the Wharton School. In the past, young men who attended these universities were generally from the rich and powerful classes and were sought after because of their family and business connections which, it was hoped, would bring more and better business into the bank. This, as would be expected, still holds true today, although the demands made upon these men and women are much more exacting and sometimes quite formidable. The training of such an account officer was conducted on a one-to-one basis under the benevolent eye of a senior officer and was carefully watched by top management. These men, and they were all men, made up the special group from which top management's successors were selected. Again, this is still substantially true today.

The operating machinery of the banking business, however, is becoming even more complex and demanding. There are highly specialized functions requiring specific aptitudes and skills that the aforesaid account officer might very well not have, nor would he have the inclination or the patience to learn. These aptitudes and skills should be sought out and reinforced by intensive technical training, and the people involved should receive the same consideration and respect accorded the account officers. No matter how much profitable business is brought into a bank, it will be as if it never had been brought in if the bank does not have the proper operating machinery to process it or competent people to run the machinery.

WHAT MANAGEMENT EXPECTED FROM AUDITING

In view of the rigid, autocratic, and regimented world in which bank employees were working, it is not surprising that management would make unrealistic demands on the auditor. They tied his hands by making him report to the same people he audited, thus denying him independence of thought and action, and by failing to give him any authority over the development and management of his function. Even worse, management made the audit function serve as an operating control, which identified it with the operation it was intended to critique. The words "audit control," which are still mistakenly used, speak for themselves. There is no such thing as audit control possible in the sense that it was used in the past. Audit is not an operating control. The audit function does not control in that sense.

To fully understand the significance of the words "audit control" as they were used, it is necessary to look at the type of coverage provided by the audit function before its real purpose was properly interpreted and actively pursued. The auditor of the past was expected to discover every error and uncover every fraud, no matter how his activities were restricted or his budget curtailed. It is interesting to note how the audit function was manipulated in the hope of achieving these impossible and unconstructive objectives.

There was hardly an auditing program in existence that did not include complete sets of duplicate records of those functions that seemed to lend themselves to an approach that would audit every transaction—uncover every error and every fraud. To maintain these duplicate records, operating departments were required to send copies of daily transaction tickets to the auditing department so that the records might be updated. Transaction tickets, essentially debits and credits, were carbonized, multiple-fanfold tickets, and one of the copies was certain to bear the preprinted legend, "Auditing Department Copy," or even more ridiculous, "Audit Control Copy." The utter futility and wastefulness of this procedure was not apparent to the auditing fraternity, which could not have done anything about it anyway. There was no open expression of opinion about the auditing mission, what its guiding philosophy should be or how its objectives, once identified and agreed upon, could be accomplished. Obviously, these duplicate records could not be maintained forever on a timely basis (they were beginning to slip), and what were they accomplishing? In defense of the auditor of the past, it must be emphasized again that he was not the articulate, independent auditor of today. He was, in a sense, a tool of management, who did not understand the nature of the internal audit function and who, in truth, "looked down their noses" at the auditor. There is no question, of course, that even today the auditor exists only if management approves and understands. Nothing exists in an organization if management does not consent. However, it is a very different ball game today. Management has every regulatory agency as well as a much better informed public looking over its shoulder. Auditors were nevertheless beginning to get together to discuss the purpose of their function, how it might be carried out, and how they could bring their story to management. The organization that eventually led this effort to a successful conclusion was the National Association of Bank Auditors and Comptrollers, established in 1924.

The main thrust of the audit function at this time was to find and correct errors, a fire-fighting operation. Prevention of error and fraud as a guiding principle or philosophy was still to come. There must have been auditors who asked themselves why errors occurred, particularly if there were definite patterns of error, or if there were not a better way of doing things. Was there, for instance, a more efficient and effective system for accounting for commercial loans, for processing the purchases and sales of securities for the bank's trust department and its other customers, or for any other function? Were these systems properly controlled to prevent loss caused by error (negligence) or fraud? Would these controls help to detect loss?

Thus auditing coverage in the past consisted primarily of finding and correcting errors, maintaining duplicate records in the hope of finding errors, performing functions that were really the responsibilities of the accounting and operating areas of the bank, and conducting the annual Directors' Examination required by most states and by the Comptroller of the Currency in the case of national banks. In retrospect, what it amounted to was that management maintained the facade of an auditing function, at the same time having some semblance of the controls it should have had anyway, with or without an auditing department. The auditor therefore was doing double duty, operating on both sides of the fence. The banking community's complacency was soon to be disturbed by events over which it would have no control, and when the following partial list of earlier auditing duties is reviewed and evaluated, the eventual, inevitable upheaval will not come as a surprise.

Some of the duplicate records maintained and operating functions performed by the auditing department were:

1   Monitoring of the changes in the bank's own investment portfolio, verification of the collection of income due, and computation of the profits and losses on the investments.

2   Maintenance of the bank's securities control general ledger, which is comparable to the general ledger account for cash, but which cannot be reflected on the official general ledger because it has no place on the bank's financial statement. Despite this, it often represents value far in excess of a bank's total worth, value for which the bank is accountable to its trust customers, its custodian, and other individual and corporate customers. It reflects in units, rather than dollars, the total amount of securities for which the bank has assumed responsibility. It does include one exception to the statement that this value has no place on the bank's financial statement, and that is the unit value of the bank's own investment portfolio. The investments of a bank are of course part of the bank's assets and are recorded on the bank's general ledger, but at book value rather than in units. The securities control general ledger is really a continuing control record of the flow of securities into and out of the bank, and unit value is the most convenient method of monitoring this flow.

3   Daily reconciliation of cash deposited in other banks to pay for the services performed by those banks for the

depositing banks. These accounts are known as ''Nostro Accounts'' and the balances are referred to as compensating balances.

4   Daily reconciliation of the bank's deposits with the Federal Reserve Bank, which as a member of the Federal Reserve System, the depositing bank is required to maintain.

5   Daily review of and follow-up on all overdrafts.

6   Daily review of all loan transactions, including new and paid-up loans and loan collateral.

7   Daily review of customers' complaints, which covered all areas of the bank. Complaints were resolved and customers received written notices of the outcome.

8   Processing of all requests by customers and their accountants as well as requests from regional bank examiners for statements of their assets and liabilities.

9   Complete audit of all trust cash and securities statements, both personal trust and employee benefit trust, before mailing them to beneficiaries, co-trustees, donors, and employee benefit trust customers.

10   Daily review of all foreign exchange transactions.

11   Physical verification and reconciliation to proven control records of all securities under bank control.

12   Counting of all cash held by each teller in his or her position as well as their reserves held in the vault.

13   Physical counting and proof to proven control records of all unissued pass books, official checks, unissued letters of credit, and other items representing potential value.

Some of these audit functions are still performed today and with good reason. Such audit functions as the physical verification of securities under vault control and processing control and cash counts are very necessary because these items are extremely susceptible to theft, fraud, burglary, and armed robbery.

In addition to the above, auditors were often stationed on a more or less permanent basis in various areas of the bank, such as the general cage on the banking floor in the main office and in the branches, the securities control section in the trust department, and other areas where physical value passed continuously through the hands of employees. The auditor checked the transactions as they were processed and reviewed the daily proofs. This practice caused the auditor to identify with the operating personnel and, ultimately, to lose his objectivity. In turn, the operating personnel tended to rely on the auditor to find their mistakes and to assist in the daily work. This inevitably led to the weakening of existing controls by encouraging laxity on the part of both operating personnel and management. The auditor became, in effect, the control that should have resided in the operating system and been monitored and enforced by management.

MANAGEMENT'S RELIANCE ON OUTSIDE AUDITORS

There are two major groups of outside auditors, regulatory or bank examiners and certified public accountants. The regulatory examiners include state banking department bank examiners, Federal Reserve Bank bank examiners, the National Bank Examiners who serve under the Comptroller of the Currency and examine national banks, and the Federal Deposit Insurance Corporation bank examiners. State-chartered banks that are members of the Federal Reserve System are examined by the Federal Reserve Bank examiners as well as by their own state banking department examiners. Certified public accountants are self-explanatory. Who has not heard of Price Waterhouse & Co.?

The essential difference between internal and outside bank auditors, aside from the fact that the former are employees of the bank, lies in their respective purposes or objectives. Internal bank auditors are concerned primarily with preventing and detecting loss. Loss may be the result of negligence (incompetence) or outright fraud. How the internal bank auditor goes about guarding against negligence and fraud is really what this book is all about.

Outside auditors, the regulatory examiners, and the certified public accountants have one thing in common: an overriding interest in the financial soundness of the bank, the competence of its management, its compliance with applicable statutory laws and regulations, the adequacy and effectiveness of its internal auditing program, and the competence of the auditor responsible for that program.

State Examiners, Federal Reserve Examiners, and National Bank Examiners usually have three separate groups of specialized examiners for commercial banking, fiduciary functions, and electronic data processing. They normally conduct their examinations on an annual basis, except for the Comptroller of the Currency, who schedules three examinations in a two-year period. He has the authority to examine a bank more frequently if in his opinion it is warranted. In New York State and very likely in other states, the Federal Reserve and State Banking Department Examiners arrange to go into a bank together to minimize the burden on the operating and auditing departments of the bank. They normally use the auditing department as their base of operation, and for very good reasons. First of all, the records and reports of all internal audits and examinations since their last visit are housed in the auditing department; second, the auditor can and does pave the way for them before they visit the different departments and divisions; third, they need a place to work on their plans and papers and to lock them away securely; and fourth, they need to discuss their findings from time to time with the auditing staff, which is beneficial to both the outside examiners and the internal auditors.

Certified public accountants are hired by banks to certify

the fairness and accuracy of their annual statements of condition. To do this with any degree of confidence, they usually spend about six months of each calendar year at the bank and use the auditing departments for exactly the same reasons the regulatory examiners do.

Since neither regulatory examiners nor certified public accountants can spend enough time within an organization to substitute for an ongoing function such as an internal auditing program, they ought not to be relied upon by management as a substitute. Further, since they are primarily interested in the financial soundness of the bank, they concentrate on the quality of the earning assets of the bank, the caliber of management, and, because they themselves are acutely aware of their natural limitations, the quality of the internal auditing program and the scope and depth of coverage. They review the schedule of audits, the reports, the findings, and the recommended corrective action taken to make certain that they may indeed rely upon the audit coverage as support for their certification or opinion.

There should be very close communication between the outside and internal auditors. Each group has something to learn from the other, and the bank is the beneficiary.

BANKING AND AUDITING IN TRANSITION AFTER WORLD WAR II

Before World War II, internal bank auditing was forced by circumstances to spend most of its time on curing the symptoms instead of the disease. Although auditors were becoming aware that this approach could not go on forever, they were only beginning to realize their strength as a developing profession. However, changes were in the wind, and internal bank auditors were soon to have their work cut out for them.

In the years that followed World War II, new and dynamic forces were hard at work churning up the industrial, financial, and social environment. The disastrous set of wars in Europe and the Pacific, both won at a staggering cost in lives, money, and morale, unleashed great tides of social and political reform along with a voracious demand for the good things in life. Many enormous undertakings were in progress: the rebuilding of war-torn cities abroad, the reconstruction of whole societies, and the long, slow healing of the wounds of war.

It is a melancholy reality that wars do more than ignite the flames of destruction. History bears witness to the fact that military needs activate the scientific and technological genius demanded to wage successful war. This is particularly true in modern times, as was seen on a gigantic scale during World War II. The humanitarian (believe it or not) and industrial progress emanating from that overpowering technological and scientific advancement opened up fantastic new industries, new markets, and untold numbers of new jobs. The increasing use of automation in business and finance created an ever-growing demand for new and highly specialized skills, many of which, happily, could be acquired without a college education. The banking industry was and is one of the prime users of automation and provided many openings for skills of this kind.

All of this promoted a universal demand for social change, a higher standard of living, and of course higher salaries to acquire this higher standard. People who in the past considered themselves chained to their jobs ventured forth into new ones. The revolving doors began spinning in banking and haven't stopped since.

BANKING'S RESPONSE TO CHANGE

Faced with the growing demand for goods, services, and financing, banking was propelled into a highly competitive environment it had not experienced before. It met this demand and competition with a rash of new services, some directed at the consumer market, some at domestic and foreign industry, and some at the correspondent banking industry.

This unprecedented growth and diversification in banking services and the development of the complex operating machinery needed to support them caused certain characteristics of present-day banking and business to emerge that, although they should have been expected, have continued to be both a threat and a challenge to management. Because banking's chief product is service, banking is finding it more difficult to isolate and control these problems, which can be generally described as follows:

1   The need to decentralize functions and segment their underlying operations to serve the burgeoning, diversified markets.
2   The ever-widening gap between top management and subordinate management levels because of this intensified specialization.
3   The inevitable inability of management to bridge this gap and stay informed.
4   The resulting impossibility of maintaining control over many greatly decentralized and segmented operations.

Banking began to recognize an urgent need for impartial and informed appraisals of its accounting, operating, and control systems and procedures. It needed to know that it could rely on the information provided by its accounting, operating, and control records, and that it would be informed of weaknesses in systems and controls that could lead to loss either from innocent error or from fraud, embezzlement, or theft. Thus the role of the modern auditor began to take shape. He was to become the eyes and ears of management.

WHAT MANAGEMENT EXPECTS FROM THE AUDITING FUNCTION TODAY

It had become painfully obvious that the old auditing approaches of maintaining duplicate records, verifying every transaction, and performing basic accounting and operating functions would not make the auditor useful to management or help to safeguard the bank. Things were moving too fast and the volume was too great. Any successful manufacturing organization knows that with high volume, not every item produced can be examined or tested. Quality control is part of the answer; the other is to provide the best equipment, the best systems, and the best people to man them. What management needs in an auditor is an informed, skilled observer who can analyze its functions and their underlying systems and procedures. Management needs an auditor who is also a banker with a need to contribute to the profit picture, one who can weigh the risks in order to set priorities and decide whether the cost of auditing outweighs the risk.

The auditor must make certain that the bank's accounting, operating, and control systems provide maximum assurance that the bank's assets are accurately recorded and safeguarded; that liabilities are properly accounted for; that income is collected and recorded; that expenses are in line, authorized, and accounted for; that the bank is complying with applicable banking law and regulations; that bank policies are being followed; and that personnel are following prescribed procedures. The auditor must also be constantly on the alert for situations, deviations from policy and procedure, and improper use of authority that might lead to loss.

WHAT AUDITING EXPECTS AND NEEDS FROM MANAGEMENT

The auditor's position in the bank's reporting structure has always been a subject of controversy. In the past ten years, however, that controversy has been subsiding, and hopefully, now that internal bank auditing has earned the status of a full-fledged profession and the respect of the banking, accounting, and financial world, that controversy will cease. There are some, however, who say that the auditor should report to the bank's board of directors through a Directors' Examining and Audit Committee; others say the auditor should report to the chairman of the board through the same committee, the latter to be composed of outside directors. Reporting to the chairman through a directors' committee is the situation to be found in most large commercial banks, and it is almost always provided for in the bylaws of the bank. It ensures the independence of the auditing function by freeing the auditor from the personal and political entanglements with banking operations. It is also the arrangement usually preferred by regulatory authorities.

There are also those who contend that the directors are too removed from operations and accounting to properly evaluate the auditor's report or to judge the quality of the internal auditing program. Therefore, they believe that the auditor should report to the controller, who has responsibility for maintaining the bank's accounting system. However, the auditor would be hard pressed to escape reviewing and appraising that system in almost any banking audit. It certainly makes sense for the auditor to feel free to contribute to the improvement of the accounting system whenever there is anything constructive to be said. Reporting to the controller might not make for a workable relationship or a happy one for the auditor.

The independence of the auditor means many things, but it does not mean that he or she is not accountable to management, nor that the auditor may ride roughshod over any person, department, or division. What it does mean is that the auditor must be free to express valid and substantiated opinions of operations, including its systems and management, without fear of reprisal; that the auditor may cross jurisdictional lines with impunity; and that the auditor is free to audit or examine any area of the bank. It means that as long as the auditor is competent, dedicated, and honest, works well with people, and is respected by the staff as a whole, he or she deserves the unqualified support of management. Moreover, that support should be a matter of record.

It would be rather difficult to argue with the statement that a bank's board of directors is responsible for providing stable and profitable administration of the bank as well as safe and controlled operations. It is also common knowledge that legally, directors are financially liable to the extent of their personal fortunes for loss caused by their negligence or their fraudulent activities. In view of this formidable responsibility and because the directors are truly removed from the details of operation, it would seem that they would seek out the auditor as an advisor and aid. In fact, this does actually describe the auditor's position today and degree of respect accorded the well-qualified and industrious auditor.

2

The Nature of
the Control
Function

HOW IT IS DEFINED

For different people, different images or interpretations are conjured up by the word "control"; to some degree, these images or interpretations are prompted by the individual's conditioning, environment, and occupation. A housewife and mother might think in terms of controlling and directing her children and her husband, a businessman in terms of controlling his employees and his expenses, a policeman in terms of controlling crime; the list could go on and on. In this discussion, we are interested in what control means to management, to bankers, and especially to the internal auditing profession.

Dictionary definitions are often surprising in the degree to which they hit the target in specialized industries as demonstrated by Webster, where control is defined as "to exercise directing, guiding or restraining power," and by the Oxford Universal Dictionary, which defines control as:

1   The fact of controlling and directing action; domination, command, sway.
2   Restraint, check.
3   To check, verify, and hence to regulate.
4   To call to account; reprove.

Of all the dictionary definitions, Webster's has the greatest application in the world of business and finance. The significance of this definition to management is more fully understood when management's urgent need for comprehensive control is clarified and appreciated.

MANAGEMENT'S NEED FOR CONTROL

Top management is directly responsible for providing sound, safe, and profitable administration of the bank's business. To accomplish this effectively, it must "exercise directing, guiding and restraining power'' over those executives to whom it has given the responsibility and commensurate authority to carry out the functions of the bank.

Management must make certain that these executives are fulfilling their obligations competently and prudently, that they are acting within the bank's policies and guidelines, and that they are complying with applicable banking laws and regulations. To function, management must delegate responsibility and authority, but it does so with the knowledge that it remains ultimately responsible and accountable to stockholders and depositors for its actions, and legally liable for loss caused by its negligence. Bad judgment can be construed as negligence.

In more specific terms, management must:

1 Be assured that the daily work will be processed accurately, efficiently, and in a timely manner.
2 Be able to rely on the financial and operating records of the bank for reporting and decision making purposes.
3 Make certain that the assets of the bank are physically safe and accurately accounted for on the official records of the bank, which must also accurately reflect the bank's liabilities.
4 Be able to ensure the implementation of its plans and the achievement and evaluation of its objectives.
5 Be able to satisfy the regulatory authorities and the bank's certified public accountants.

There are other factors which complicate the problem of control and make its implementation even more difficult. They challenge the imagination and the ingenuity of both top management and operations.

The worlds of business, finance, and government have been exploding at an exponential rate and have created an unprecedented demand for specialization in every area of banking. As a result, the inevitable decentralization and segmentation of banking functions and operations, aggravated by the deluge of legal requirements and paper work created by federal and state laws and agencies, have served to produce an ever-widening gap between management and its operations. This has made close supervision impossible, at least in most medium- and large-sized banks. It has created almost insurmountable problems in communications. Operating management and personnel cannot comprehend management's dilemma, and management, because of tremendous pressures, has generally assigned an unrealistic and dangerously low priority to the needs of its operations management and personnel.

Considering all the responsibilities of management, its critical need for reliable information, and its obligation to direct and control in the face of the obstacles impeding it, many questions arise which demand satisfactory answers. Some of the most urgent appear to be the following:

1   What controls should management be able to rely on?
2   How do they function?
3   How can management be sure they are always functioning properly?
4   How can management be certain that it is being kept accurately informed at all times about the condition of its operations and the effectiveness of its underlying controls?

The answers to these questions reside in the overall control structure and its component parts.

THE CONTROL FUNCTION AND ITS COMPONENT SYSTEMS OF CONTROL

Managerial Control

The organization or reporting structure of a bank is, in essence, the master control system that coordinates the highly decentralized and segmented operations of modern banking. It is the foundation of an integrated network of accounting, operating, and other systems of internal control which make it possible for management to achieve its primary objective of safe, efficient, and profitable banking operations.

As the master system of managerial control, the organizational structure, if established in accordance with sound principles, provides for the delegation of responsibility and commensurate authority as well as accountability for all action taken under the authority granted. It provides direction and guidance to all levels of management from the highest to the lowest, and requires upward reporting from the lowest levels up to the top.

It is quite clear that there is a very real need for the services of a disinterested observer, someone who has a thorough knowledge of banking functions and operations as well as banking policies, procedures, and regulations. This observer must also be an experienced systems analyst and an effective communicator. To put it another way, management needs the services of a seasoned liaison and control officer to facilitate the coordination and direction of their expanded operations. This control officer would play a key role in the bank's managerial control system by keeping management informed as to the adequacy and effectiveness of its accounting and operating systems and their supporting systems of control.

From time to time there has been heated controversy over the question of who should have the position of control officer. Throughout the years, some have contended that the controller or some other financial officer should have that position. The consensus of current opinion, however, is that a qualified internal auditor whose independence is guaranteed under the bylaws and who commands the respect and full support of management is the one person who could most effectively fill this role.

It is much easier to understand both the organization or reporting structure of a bank and the position of the internal

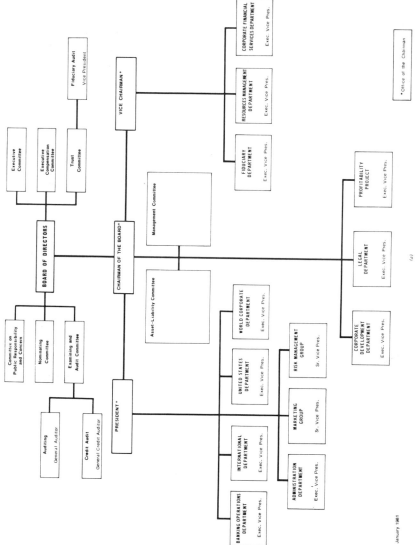

BOARD OF DIRECTORS

Executive Committee
Executive Compensation Committee
Trust Committee
Fiduciary Audit — Vice President

Committee on Public Responsibility and Concern
Nominating Committee
Examining and Audit Committee

Auditing — General Auditor
Credit Audit — General Credit Auditor

CHAIRMAN OF THE BOARD*

Management Committee
Asset-Liability Committee

VICE CHAIRMAN*

FIDUCIARY DEPARTMENT — Exec. Vice Pres.
RESOURCES MANAGEMENT DEPARTMENT — Exec. Vice Pres.
CORPORATE FINANCIAL SERVICES DEPARTMENT — Exec. Vice Pres.

PRESIDENT*

BANKING OPERATIONS DEPARTMENT — Exec. Vice Pres.
INTERNATIONAL DEPARTMENT — Exec. Vice Pres.
UNITED STATES DEPARTMENT — Exec. Vice Pres.
WORLD CORPORATE DEPARTMENT — Exec. Vice Pres.

ADMINISTRATION DEPARTMENT — Exec. Vice Pres.
MARKETING GROUP — Sr. Vice Pres.
RISK MANAGEMENT GROUP — Sr. Vice Pres.

CORPORATE DEVELOPMENT DEPARTMENT — Exec. Vice Pres.
LEGAL DEPARTMENT — Exec. Vice Pres.
PROFITABILITY PROJECT — Exec. Vice Pres.

*Office of the Chairman

January 1981

(a)

30

auditor as the control officer in this master managerial system of control by studying the organizational chart of an actual bank. The broad organizational chart of Bankers Trust Company is reproduced here. The bank's managerial control system at the top levels is clearly defined, as is the reporting status of the General Auditor and the General Credit Auditor, who work closely together on the problems involved in the audit of the lending function and the supporting loan operating and control systems. Because of the critical nature of the lending function, many banks have seen fit to have a specialized credit auditor. They are both responsible to the Chairman of the Board and to the Board of Directors through the Examining and Audit Committee, which is composed solely of directors who are not also officers of the bank. All of these requirements are set forth quite specifically in the bylaws of the bank.

The Fiduciary Audit function shown at the upper-right-hand side is not an independent audit function such as that performed by the General Auditor. It is carried out by the Fiduciary Department itself, which audits or reviews its own performance. The person in charge is an officer of the Fiduciary Department who reports to the Fiduciary Committee and not to the Chairman of the Board.

The accompanying reproduction of the organizational chart of the Banking Operations Department shows its further subdivisions or groups and the two subordinate levels of management in each group. Although there is no chart to illustrate them, even further subdivisions and lower subordinate management levels are not difficult to visualize. These lower management levels, contrary to some current opinion, are often just as critical as some higher levels. More attention should be paid by many banks to these lower levels. Each level, from the lowest to the highest, has its own responsibilities and authority—or should have—and should be accountable to the next higher level. At any level, if something goes wrong, it could affect the entire operation.

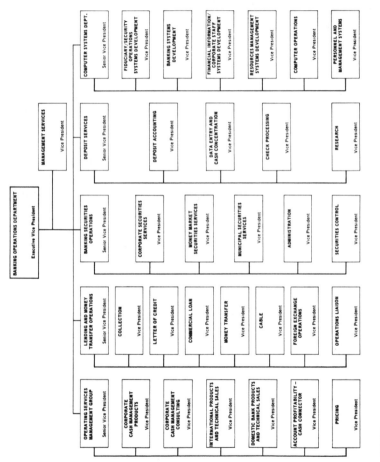

BANKING OPERATIONS DEPARTMENT
Executive Vice President

MANAGEMENT SERVICES
Vice President

OPERATING SERVICES MANAGEMENT GROUP
Senior Vice President
- CORPORATE CASH MANAGEMENT PRODUCTS — Vice President
- CORPORATE CASH MANAGEMENT CONSULTING — Vice President
- INTERNATIONAL PRODUCTS AND TECHNICAL SALES — Vice President
- DOMESTIC BANK PRODUCTS AND TECHNICAL SALES — Vice President
- ACCOUNT PROFITABILITY – CASH CONNECTOR — Vice President
- PRICING — Vice President

LENDING AND MONEY TRANSFER OPERATIONS
Senior Vice President
- COLLECTION — Vice President
- LETTER OF CREDIT — Vice President
- COMMERCIAL LOAN — Vice President
- MONEY TRANSFER — Vice President
- CABLE — Vice President
- FOREIGN EXCHANGE OPERATIONS — Vice President
- OPERATIONS LIAISON — Vice President

BANKING SECURITIES OPERATIONS
Senior Vice President
- CORPORATE SECURITIES SERVICES — Vice President
- MONEY MARKET SECURITIES SERVICES — Vice President
- MUNICIPAL SECURITIES SERVICES — Vice President
- ADMINISTRATION — Vice President
- SECURITIES CONTROL — Vice President

DEPOSIT SERVICES
Senior Vice President
- DEPOSIT ACCOUNTING — Vice President
- DATA ENTRY AND CASH CONCENTRATION — Vice President
- CHECK PROCESSING — Vice President
- RESEARCH — Vice President

COMPUTER SYSTEMS DEPT.
Senior Vice President
- FIDUCIARY/SECURITY OPERATIONS SYSTEMS DEVELOPMENT
- BANKING SYSTEMS DEVELOPMENT — Vice President
- FINANCIAL INFORMATION/CORPORATE STAFF SYSTEMS DEVELOPMENT — Vice President
- RESOURCES MANAGEMENT SYSTEMS DEVELOPMENT — Vice President
- COMPUTER OPERATIONS — Vice President
- PERSONNEL AND MANAGEMENT SYSTEMS — Vice President

January 1981

32

Each one should be regarded as a building block in the overall system.

The corporate management structure is obviously an excellent vehicle for the exercise of effective control, at least from the point of view of managerial control. Accounting and operating control systems are, broadly speaking, parallel structures that utilize the managerial control system to implement their own requirements. It would seem that very little could stand in the way of almost perfect control of all functions and their accounting and operating systems. It is a frustrating fact of life, however, that even the most perfect of systems is almost totally dependent upon people. People, in turn, are critically dependent upon timely and effective communication. People are also fallible, and people at different management levels have different perspectives. Unfortunately, top management's attention is diverted by far too many extraneous demands, and as a result, it has been forced to set what it believes are justifiable priorities. Some are justifiable in light of extreme outside pressures, but some, from a practical business viewpoint, are not.

Who is the right person to advise management that some things should be assigned a higher priority or that management has not been accurately informed about the condition of the bank's systems and controls? Only someone whose job requires that he or she do just that. This is without question the responsibility of the internal auditor. It should be kept in mind, however, that the internal auditor must be a uniquely qualified individual, and therein might lie a problem. Not every internal auditor can effectively fill this role, either by virtue of official status or of personal qualifications and experience. The internal auditor is a facet of managerial control and as such must be able to understand management's objectives and its obligation to exercise prudent judgment in its assumption of risk. The internal auditor must be able to assist management in these functions, at the same time fulfilling his or her obligation to protect the safety of the bank's operations.

Other Major Systems of Internal Control

All systems of control are commonly referred to in the internal auditing and accounting professions as "internal controls." This of course is quite correct because they are all internal. There are, however, several types of internal controls. One, managerial control, has just been discussed. The others are accounting controls, financial controls, operating controls, and a group of specialized internal controls that have almost universal applicability. All banking systems involve the use of all four.

Accounting Controls

The bank's system of accounting and its supporting control system are closely related to the organizational structure of the bank and they are the chief responsibility of the controller. Through this system flow all the debits and credits from all areas of the bank affecting the asset, liability, capital, income, and expense accounts on the bank's general ledger. The bank's annual reports, other periodic financial statements, tax returns, reports for regulatory authorities and bank examiners, as well as management information reports are prepared from the data in these accounts. Operating areas also use the data in some of these accounts in the course of their daily work. At any given time, therefore, the data must be accurate and up to date. Management must be able to rely on them absolutely and the auditor must make the reliability of the data one of auditing's primary concerns if the auditing objective of preventing and detecting loss is to be achieved.

Accounting controls, which are essentially a series of proofs and checks and balances between sending and receiving areas, and between these areas and the general ledger, are critically important in every department and division of the bank. It is one of the major responsibilities of all managers at every level to make certain that all accounting procedures are spelled out in detail and in writing and that they are being followed faithfully, without exception. All entries affect the subsidiary and major accounts on the general ledger and, of course, the resulting data used in official reports.

All departments, divisions, and branches pass daily entries to the bank's general ledger and should maintain a daily record of these entries. A record such as this is usually called a daily journal, which in substance is a categorized summary and proof of all of the day's debits and credits, supported by copies of the individual entries affecting the various accounts on the general ledger. The original tickets along with the original copy of the journal or proof sheet are sent to the general ledger for posting. Basically, the same procedure should be followed where there are interdivisional entries, entries between branches, or entries between branches and divisions. Sending and receiving areas must prove with each other and with the general ledger.

Many departments and divisions as well as branches maintain subsidiary accounting records that tie in with the general ledger and must be kept in proof on a daily basis. The commercial loan department and the bond or investment department are important examples because they are responsible for major earning assets and their departmental records must be accurate at all times.

The review, analysis, and appraisal of accounting controls is a primary responsibility of the internal auditor, who is also responsible for the safety of the bank's assets. During audits and examinations, the internal auditor must constantly be alert to any weakness or deterioration in accounting controls or to any departure from approved accounting procedures and policy.

Financial Controls

These are the products or end results of the bank's accounting and control systems that are used by management and others to monitor its progress in the marketplace and its financial position. It is most important, for example, for management to know what it is earning on its loans and other investments and whether or not its other services are profitable. These are but a few of the many aspects of the bank's financial performance that management must track, and which it does from the data provided by the bank's accounting records.

Operating Controls

Operating controls are fifficult to define because they are dependent upon the nature and complexity of the system they are designed to protect. Operating controls are really a mixture of accounting controls, managerial controls, and the checks and balances built into an operating system to promote safe, accurate, and timely processing of all transactions. Safety of processing means the prevention and detection of loss caused by negligence or fraud. Each operating system is designed and constructed to carry out the work of a specific function or service, and therefore is different from all other systems. It follows, of course, that interwoven systems of controls must be designed to suit the requirements of each individual operating system.

"Checks and balances" are convenient labels used to describe internal operating controls that are not necessarily accounting or managerial controls but are critical to the safety and accuracy of the processing. Some of the more strategic and effective "checks and balances" are discussed next.

Segregation of Duties

This control is one of the most effective safeguards against internal fraud and sometimes against a combination of internal and external fraud as well as against innocent error. It must of course be well planned and strictly enforced. All controls, by the way, are effective only if they are enforced and this is where one of the facets of managerial control—supervision and communication—comes into play. The purpose of this control is to prevent a single individual from handling a transaction alone from its inception on through to its completion. A readily understood illustration of the need for segregation of duties would be a teller who handles deposits, withdrawals, check cashing, and other duties incidental to the job of a teller and is also permitted to post these transactions to the individual account ledgers, sometimes even to the bank's general ledger. In a situation such as this, the teller is in an ideal position to divert funds to his or her own use and then to cover up the theft by fraudulent manipulation of the accounting records.

Banking and trust functions and operations are rich in opportunities for implementing segregation of duties. It is, however, expensive because it requires an adequate staff. A small bank therefore would have difficulty in using this control and would tend to depend on the auditor as a substitute control.

The trust department of a bank is particularly vulnerable to fraud because it exercises discretion in managing the assets of trusts and estates as if it were the owner. It is always in the process of buying and selling securities, and of collecting and disbursing funds. The trust officer is responsible for issuing instructions for the distribution of income and/or principal to trust beneficiaries, and of estate assets to heirs or legatees. The trust officer should not be allowed to actually issue or sign the checks. Rather, the trust department should have a special disbursement section where the trust officer's instructions are verified, the checks are issued, and another officer or designated employee signs them. There have been many instances in which trust officers have helped themselves to these funds without anyone's knowing about it for a long time. There is another sometimes overlooked opportunity for a trust or investment officer to defraud a trust in the exercise of the investment function. This officer should not be permitted to deal directly with the brokers, because the officer and the broker's representative could act in collusion to steal from the principal of the trust. Everyone is aware that securities fluctuate on the market during any trading day. The officer and the broker's representative could agree to record purchases at the high of the day the trade was made, when actually the purchase was made at a lower price. They could then charge the trust for the higher price and split the difference between them. Acutally, this requires a considerable amount of record manipulation, but it can and has been done. Instructions to buy or sell should be given to traders to execute; they in turn should transmit these instructions to the securities processing department to process and either pay for or receive the proceeds.

Dual Control

This is actually a continuing verification by one or more people of what has already been done by someone else. For example, dual control exists in a situation in which the first person prepares a bill for a banking service performed and initials it, and a second person verifies it and approves it. In a continuing processing stream where a transaction must pass from one station to another, each succeeding processor is in the position of having to verify what the previous processor has done. If one or more processors fail to do this and the requirement is not enforced, then the processors at the particular stations are negligent, as is the officer or manager in charge.

Joint Custody

Joint custody is a form of dual control, but a very specialized form. It exists where two or more people hold items of value in safekeeping. The most well-recognized example of this control is the joint custody of the bank vault. Normally, a senior vault officer holds one half of the combination lock of the vault and another officer of the bank holds the other half. It is important that neither officer finds out the other half of the combination. Both of course must be present to open the vault at the opening of business each day. The bank vault holds securities belonging to estates, personal trusts, employee benefit trusts (pension, profit sharing, and savings incentive trusts), and customers who have designated the bank as custodian of their own investment portfolios. These customers are usually other banks, insurance companies, industrial corporations, individuals, and federal, state, and local government agencies.

Among other items of value that should be held in joint custody are reserve cash, collateral held to secure loans, unissued official checks, unissued E bonds, and unissued stock and bond certificates. Safe deposit boxes rented by the public arc always held under the joint custody of the lessee and the vault officer, both of whom must participate in opening the safe-deposit box.

Rotation of Employees

This can be very beneficial both for management and the employees if it is carried out in accordance with a carefully thought out plan. It can also be most destructive to employee morale, thus defeating management's objectives, if it is done carelessly and without regard for the employees' sense of personal dignity and desire for a career path.

Rotating employees' assignments within a division or department in accordance with a thoughtfully designed plan can accomplish several things:

1 It can uncover fraudulent activities, loss, error, and departures from approved procedures.
2 It can bring to light hidden backlogs of work still to be processed.
3 It can create a staff of well-trained and well-rounded people capable of performing many functions and even-

tually supervising the work of the section, division, or department.

4   It can enhance the morale of the staff, thus improving the quality of the work, because the employees can anticipate their upward progress as a result of the cross training they have been given.

Mandatory Vacations

This is closely allied to rotation of employees. Its purpose should be obvious: to disclose any fraudulent activities on the part of officers and other employees. Normally, all employees, especially officers, should be required to take two consecutive weeks of vacation away from the bank premises and any contact with fellow employees or officers. This should provide sufficient time for any fraud or illegal activity to surface because the vacationing perpetrator is not there to protect his or her interests.

Accrual Accounting

This control was once referred to by a much-respected banker and teacher as "sugar bowl accounting." He explained that his mother took his father's weekly pay and portioned it off into various old sugar bowls for rent, gas, electricity, and so forth. This of course only took care of household expenses, but the principle was clear. Income is not earned and expenses are not always incurred at the time the cash is received or paid out. If a bank or any organization were to account for its earnings when they were actually received, or for most of its expenses when they were actually paid, the bank's true earnings picture would be sadly distorted. Earnings on loans, investments, and services accrue on a daily basis, but are usually received long after they have been earned; fixed expenses, on the other hand, are usually paid long before they are incurred. Spreading this out on the accounting records over the earning and expense periods makes great sense. It helps to present a more accurate picture of the bank's earnings and expenses. However, being on an accrual rather than a cash basis has two other great advantages. That is, it provides for control of anticipated earnings and expenses, and it facilitates planning for future expenditures.

Accrual accounting is a rare combination of an accounting, operating, and managerial control.

Controls should be used with insight and prudence. Experience is of course invaluable in this respect. Undercontrolled systems are dangerous, but so are overcontrolled systems, because bottlenecks and log jams can kill an operation. Banking is not comparable to other industries because its assets are not totally its own. It uses depositors' funds to create the assets needed to earn money to keep the bank afloat, to pay dividends to stockholders, and to pay interest. That is why banking is such a highly regulated industry and why effectively controlled operations are needed and demanded by federal and state regulatory authorities.

The establishment of control systems is the responsibility of the bank's operating management, and it is the auditor's responsibility to make certain that they are there, that they are working effectively, and that they are being enforced. However, management and the public must realize that nothing is foolproof, and that even the best of controls can be circumvented by intelligent and determined adversaries. Nevertheless, they make the perpetration of fraud more difficult and are psychological deterents to fraud and crime.

3

Banking Functions or the Scope of the Internal Bank Audit Program

The auditor as a top managerial control performs a vital service for management. If he or she is to perform this service effectively, the entire bank must be open to the auditor's analytical scrutiny and evaluation. Under ideal conditions, the bylaws of a bank provide not only for the auditor's independence but for the unlimited scope of the audit function. This is usually accomplished by a statement in the bylaws that the auditor is responsible for the safety of all operations. Although the bylaws should have the effect of guaranteeing both the auditor's freedom from all intimidation by operating management and the right to audit any and every area of a bank, it must be recognized that, realistically, the auditor also needs the respect, understanding, and strong support of top management. This will, of course, vary in accordance with the enlightened attitude and determination of management and its evaluation of the competence and strength of the auditor. It is not uncommon to see auditors restricted in their endeavors by a management that either does not fully comprehend the extent of its own potential liability or does not have the confidence in the capabilities of its auditor that it ought to have.

In the banking industry, the term "operations" may be interpreted in two different ways. Depending on the context in which it is used, it may mean only the accounting and processing systems and procedures employed in carrying out the functions and services sold to customers, or it may also encompass the policies, procedures, and legal constraints that must be observed in dealing with customers and in providing them with these services. When "operations" is used in connection with the internal auditor's responsibilities, it is all inclusive. The auditor is vitally concerned with everything involved in providing the customer with a service as well as with all the supporting operations that carry out the performance of the service. For example, the auditor is interested not only in the accounting systems and procedures supporting the recording and continuing administration of a commercial loan, but also in the degree to which a lending officer has adhered to officially approved credit policies and procedures for extending a line of credit or approving a loan, and in the applicable statutory laws and regulations. Another example is the fiduciary services offered by most large- and medium-sized banks. The auditor's concern must focus not only on the trust accounting and securities processing systems and controls, but also on the heart of fiduciary liability, which primarily depends on the proper interpretation of and compliance with the estate's or trust's governing instrument (that is, either the will or the trust agreement), and on compliance with the general law of trusts and applicable statutory laws and regulations.

The functions and services offered by banks across the country will vary because of size, regional constraints, management policies, and economic conditions, but the foregoing brief description of the extent and depth of the internal auditor's interest in all banking functions and services should give the reader at least a glimpse of the enormity of the internal bank auditing responsibility. To be responsible for the safety of all of a bank's operations is a formidable undertaking, particularly when the significance of the word "safety" is really understood. What does "safety" mean to the internal bank auditor? To the average person it probably means physical safety, but to the internal auditor and the rest of the business and financial community, the word "safety" has definite accounting, automation, legal, and physical ramifications. The internal bank auditor must not only be familiar with the technical aspects of each function and service; he must also be acutely aware of the varied liabilities inherent in each function and service.

Except for fiduciary investments and securities held in an agency capacity for custodian customers, most banking functions and services are part of one or more of the following broad classifications as they are reflected on a bank's general ledger and ultimately on its financial statement:

Assets
Liabilities and capital
Income
Expense

The purpose of this book is to define and clarify the role of the internal bank auditor, the extent and depth of the auditor's responsibility, and to convey a broad understanding of what is involved in auditing a bank. A limited emphasis therefore is being placed on the technical accounting aspects of banking functions and services, which would require a more comprehensive and detailed treatment than is possible within the constraints of this book. It is assumed that most readers understand that deposits, or customers' funds, are liabilities of a bank and are so recorded on the bank's accounting records. It is also assumed that the same readers realize that these funds are, of necessity, invested in loans, securities, and fixed assets such as business machines, computers, and buildings for the purpose of producing income. Loans, securities, and money market operations constitute the major part of a bank's earning power, and fixed assets contribute to their earning power.

A commercial bank also has nonledger liabilities in the form of personal trust and estate investments, employee benefit trust investments, corporate trust accounts, and custodian accounts. These investments are not made by a bank for its own profit but for the benefit of others and therefore are not reflected on the asset side of the general ledger. Trust assets are not assets of a bank. They are managed by a bank only for the fees or commissions provided for by wills, agreements, statutes, or a combination of the three. In most large commercial banks and in some medium-sized banks, the market value of trust assets often is larger than the total asset value of the bank. Many banks include custodian securities in their fiduciary totals.

THE DEPOSIT FUNCTION

Commercial Deposit Accounts

Commercial banks, savings banks, corporations, private entrepreneurs, charitable organizations, and government agencies (public funds) rely on banks to perform many financial services for them. These services include receiving and collecting the proceeds of checks to be deposited in their accounts, charging their accounts in payment for checks they have issued, transferring funds to other parties at their request, and housing and servicing their securities; that is, collecting and crediting their accounts with the dividends and interest due on securities, collecting and crediting their deposit accounts with the proceeds of matured securities and securities they have sold, and charging their accounts for securities they have purchased. All of these services and many more have to be paid for by the customer, usually through what are known as compensating balances; that is, balances that can produce a return high enough to cover the prices of the services rendered when invested at current rates of interest. Prices of services offered must not only cover the cost of producing the services, but must yield a competitive profit. A servicing bank is, after all, in business to earn a profit. If a customer maintains excess balances during a particular month, the earnings on the excess are usually applied to prices of services provided in the following month. If the customer's balances have been deficient, the customer compensates the bank either by sending a check for the amount due or by increasing the balances sufficiently to make up for the loss in earnings.

Banks have also devised specialized deposit services to speed up the collection of cash, increase customers' available funds, and ultimately assist customers in managing their cash positions more effectively. Customers are of course most interested in reducing the time it takes to collect checks drawn to their order and in being able to find out, almost on an hourly basis, what funds are available to them for investment and disbursement. A discussion of some of the most popular services being offered for this purpose follows.

Lock Box

Everyone is familiar with the frustration caused by Postal Service delays and by their own internal operating delays. The lock box has reduced these delays significantly. It is a relatively simple concept that has been available for years and is particularly well suited to firms that have large quantities of remittances received through the mails.

The customer rents a post office box in both its own name and the name of its bank. It also instructs its customers to send their remittances to that post office box and gives its bank the authority to pick up the box's contents. A bank usually picks up several times a day, even on weekends and holidays. The contents are then sorted at the bank, the checks and accompanying documents are microfilmed, and the customer's deposit account is credited. The checks are processed as quickly as possible for collection, and the customer receives a copy of the transactions and accompanying details so that it can update its accounts receivable promptly. If the customer's accounts receivable is automated, most banks usually can provide the information in order by account number on magnetic tape. Some banks have very sophisticated computer systems that permit their customers to access their computer files via computer terminals, which speeds up the customer's operations even further.

Zero Balance Accounts

These are special accounts maintained by customers as an adjunct to their regular deposit accounts. They are designed to facilitate a customer's disbursement function. At the end of each business day, the total of a customer's debits is zeroed out by transferring that amount from the customer's regular account to the zero balance account.

Payable Through Drafts

This service is a favorite with customers who disburse a large volume of funds from many locations. It is very similar to a check but its payment must be authorized by the issuing corporation. The bank serves as an intermediary or clearing agent. It refers the check to its issuing customer for authorization to pay, thereby protecting the customer against internal or external fraud. Insurance companies are likely to use this service for payment of claims. It is an effective disbursement control mechanism but a burdensome one to the servicing bank.

Their are many other disbursement control services available which incorporate the lock box service, payable through drafts, balance reporting, and other features such as account reconciliation and check retention. Many combinations are available and the total package can be designed to fit the customer's needs.

This is a very simplified description of commercial deposit accounts, but detailed enough so that the nonbanker can understand the basic differences between commercial deposit accounts and the special checking accounts maintained by the average individual banking customer, more familiarly known as the consumer.

Special Checking Accounts

These deposit accounts are well known to the average individual or small business banking customer. They are essentially what the name implies, a vehicle for the average customer to deposit funds against which checks may be drawn. The service is provided for a fixed fee that is composed of a monthly maintainence or bookkeeping charge and a charge for each check paid. There are also extra charges for returned items, overdrafts, and stop payments. In addition, these accounts often carry overdraft privileges, which are in effect advances or loans for which the customer pays interest at the going rate; of course, this privilege requires proper credit validation. Special checking is a service belonging to the retail banking function, whereas the commercial deposit service is part of what is known as wholesale banking. Profitable retail banking services depend on high volume and low processing costs, which normally demand a large investment in automation that some banks believe is not worthwhile.

Savings Accounts

Savings accounts require very little explanation. They have been in existence since the beginning of banking in the United States and have served the individual depositor whatever his or her economic status. It is true that in the early days, due to lack of regulation and inadequate supervision, small depositors were frequently wiped out by the manipulations of irresponsible bank management. It should be noted, however, that during the post-1929 years no mutual savings bank suffered as the commercial banks did. The Banking Act of 1933 created the Federal Deposit Insurance Corporation, which all national banks and members of the Federal Reserve System were required to join. It is probably safe to say that today all mutual savings banks, state-chartered commercial banks, and, of course, all national banks belong. Obviously, membership in the corporation is a ''must'' if banks want to attract depositors. It adds tremendously to the public's peace of mind to know that its bank deposits are insured, and helps to keep the banking industry stable during times of crisis.

Mutual savings banks have been highly regulated for

many years. So have been commercial banks, which have not been permitted to pay as much interest on savings accounts because of the advantage they enjoyed in being able to offer a much wider range of services to the individual. The once-definitive lines that distinguished the savings bank industry from commercial banking are beginning to weaken. Savings banks may now offer checking accounts and other services once restricted to commercial banks, and both industries are now competing with each other in many ways. Because of high inflation and high interest rates, mutual savings banks are presently experiencing a substantial drain on their deposits. Depositors are putting their money into the many money market funds offered by both commercial banks and large brokerage firms. These funds pay much higher rates of interest than the savings banks and still permit the participant to make withdrawals without a penalty. As such, they operate very much like checking accounts.

THE LENDING FUNCTION

The immediate and most important duty of bank management is the prudent investment of customers' deposits in earning assets. Management's dilemma is how to distribute these deposits among various types of loans, that is, commercial loans, real estate loans, installment loans, and securities. The problem, of course, is always created by the economics of the situation at any given time, which involves many factors not properly the subject of this book. Nevertheless, bank funds must be invested profitably and safely. Although loans, securities, and fixed assets are recorded on the bank's general ledger as bank assets, it must be emphasized that they are different from the assets of nonbanking businesses in that they represent money belonging to other people, the bank's depositors.

Commercial Loans

Traditionally, commercial loans, which are part of the wholesale rather than retail banking effort, have constituted the major part of a commercial bank's outstanding loans and have often been referred to as "the bread basket" of banking. Commercial loans are loans made to business enterprises, both corporate (including banks) and noncorporate, and to individuals for business financing purposes.

Commercial loans may be short-term loans, usually made for a year or less to finance a company's inventory or accounts receivable because of seasonal or other cash-flow problems. Term loans are made for periods longer than one year and are usually made to finance a large capital investment such as plant and equipment. Repayment of term loans is usually made on a periodic basis, in contrast to short-term loans, which are normally repaid at maturity from business income.

Long-term loans are made after very careful evaluation of the profitability of a particular industry or business and, of course, of the intended borrower. They are riskier than short-term loans and consequently the rate of interest charged is higher. Loans are also made on a payable-on-demand basis, which means that the loan has no predetermined maturity date and the bank may ask for repayment at any time. Demand loans are made when the bank wants to accommodate a good customer, but at the same time recognizes a risk and wants to be in control of the situation.

Short-term, term, and demand loans may be secured or unsecured. If they are secured, it means the borrower has been asked to pledge collateral, usually top-grade stocks and/or bonds, to secure the loan in the event that the borrower becomes unable to repay it.

Interest on commercial loans is usually tied into the prime rate, which is the rate that commercial banks charge their most valued customers, that is, the customers with the very best credit rating. The rise and fall of the prime rate is tied into the state of the economy, and although it warrants further, detailed discussion, is more properly the subject of another book on another topic. It should be noted, however, that individual banks control the rates of interest they charge individual customers and set them in relation to their own needs, to the value of the customer in question, and to their own expectation of what the future has in store for interest rates and their own loan investment policies.

Many commercial loans also involve extending lines of credit that in effect enable the borrower to borrow against a maximum line of credit from time to time without filing a new application each time. The bank reviews each new demand for borrowing against the line in terms of the customer's current financial condition. Naturally, the customer pays for this availability of funds. Usually, payment is in the form of a balance deposit, known as a compensating balance. This means that the customer must have on deposit enough money to yield a return sufficient to cover the line or commitment fee when invested at the current rate. The customer may also pay in "hard" dollars, which is an outright fee paid by check or by a charge to the customer's account. Compensating balances, in contrast, are known as "soft" dollars. The credit line granted may also be a revolving credit enabling the borrower to borrow several times up to the line's limit as it is reduced by interim payments.

Obviously, the bank's investigation and analysis of either a potential or actual customer must be thorough and continuing. A borrower's credit picture may change for better or for worse, or it may remain the same. A very close relationship should exist between the lending bank and the customer.

Commercial loans are preferred by banks because they are less costly to support with operating services, and although they are normally fewer in number, they are infinitely higher in dollar value. In addition, because they are negotiable at their inception and often during their existence, they usually are much more profitable insofar as interest and compensating balance features are concerned.

Installment Loans

Installment loans are a feature of retail or consumer banking and are made for many purposes. There are a number of essential differences between installment loans and commercial loans. Installment loans are individually smaller in amount. They are repayable both for interest and principal in fixed monthly amounts over periods of from one to three years. With installment loans, credit is granted in accordance with fixed conditions. Nothing is negotiable as in commercial lending. The margin of profit is smaller than in commercial lending because of high operating costs. However, the credit risk is greater because repayment depends on the borrower's salary, and therefore interest is much higher.

There are many other types of loans, including construction loans, home mortgage loans, Small Business Administration loans, and of course credit card loans and overdraft privileges on checking accounts.

The auditor must thoroughly understand all of these lending variations and others not specifically mentioned, as well as the bank's policies, procedures, and systems involved in granting these loans. The auditor must also be fully aware of the liabilities inherent in each type of lending facility.

SECURITIES SERVICES

Custodian Services

Banks, corporations, government agencies, foundations, individuals acting as executors and trustees, individuals investing for themselves, churches, and others usually rely on money center and regional banks for help in safely housing and servicing their investments. This is an agency relationship, which simply means that the customer and the servicing bank enter into a written agreement that generally provides that the servicing bank will perform the following seven functions.

1 Physically house the customer's securities in its vaults, giving them the same degree of care it gives its own investments and assuming responsibility for all losses resulting from negligence or fraud on the part of any of its employees, officers, or agents.

2 Maintain accurate records of the customer's securities and provide periodic statements of the customer's investments.

3 Upon timely instructions from the customer, receive and pay for securities purchased by the customer, or deliver to designated brokers securities the customer has sold, collect the proceeds thereof, and debit or credit the customer's cash account.

4 Present for redemption all maturing securities, collect the proceeds thereof, and credit the customer's cash account.

5 On the payable date, credit the customer's cash account for all interest and dividends due, irrespective of whether such income has actually been received by the bank (this requires a carefully monitored income collection accounting system).

6 Remit funds to the customer or other designated parties in accordance with customer's written instructions.

7 Keep the customer advised of all corporate or other issuers' financial activity (for example, tenders, mergers, or exchanges), pending in connection with the customer's holdings, and act in accordance with the customer's instructions concerning such financial activity.

It is important to understand the difference between commercial banks in money market centers and regional commercial banks to properly evaluate the significance of the custodian service. Money market centers include those major cities such as New York, Chicago, and San Francisco where the major stock exchanges and money markets are located and the bulk of the securities trading takes place. It is obvious, therefore, that corporations, banks, individuals, and others who trade on these exchanges need someone physically close to the scene and technically capable of handling their securities transactions. Rural banks go to regional banks and to the money center banks, whereas regional banks often give all of their business to the money center banks. Commercial banks in New York City receive the bulk of the nation's securities transaction business, because the majority of the transactions take place in New York City.

Although the custodian relationship is basically an agency relationship, it carries with it overtones of a fiduciary relationship, particularly in those instances where an individual executor and/or trustee enters into a custodian relationship with a bank. Courts of jurisdiction have consistently held that because the custodian bank represents itself to the public as an expert in fiduciary matters, it may not participate in any act of the individual fiduciary that violates a provision of a will, trust agreement, or applicable trust or statutory law. Normally, therefore, the custodian bank will ask the individual fiduciary for a certified copy of the will or trust agreement and have counsel review and analyze it. If the individual executor or trustee instructs the custodian bank to execute a transaction that is in violation of the governing instrument or applicable law, the custodian bank should refuse, with an explanation of its reasons for such refusal. Custodian banks participating in such transactions are legally liable for the consequences.*

*See Austin Wakeman Scott, *Scott On Trusts,* Little, Brown and Company, Boston, Mass., 1981, Sections 326.4, 326.5, 326.6.

FIDUCIARY SERVICES

A bank performs many fiduciary services. It acts as executor of decedents' estates, as trustee of personal trusts established under wills or trust agreements with living donors, as trustee of employee benefit trusts such as pension plans, profit-sharing plans, savings incentive plans, and other plans established under agreements with corporations, banks, and other business enterprises, and as trustee under corporate trust agreements. These fiduciary services are dramatically different from all other banking services. A fiduciary holds legal title to the assets of estates and of personal and employee benefit trusts, managing them as if it were the owner. The difference is that it does so for the benefit of others, that is, for the beneficiaries of estates, personal and employee benefit trusts, and remaindermen, who take the assets of a personal trust upon its termination.

Estates and Personal Trusts

Will and trust agreements, which are known as the governing instruments, confer discretionary powers upon fiduciaries and provide for the performance of specific duties. There are also many fiduciary duties implied by law because of the very special nature of the fiduciary relationship. In exercising discretionary powers and carrying out specified duties, the fiduciary must act in accordance with applicable statutory law and the General Law of Trusts.

The auditor must have an intimate knowledge of the General Law of Trusts to fully understand the nature of fiduciary liability. The General Law of Trusts is a body of principles developed by courts of equity over the centuries which have been reaffirmed consistently in major decisions since earliest times to the present day. These principles prescribe the manner in which fiduciaries should carry out their explicit duties and their discretionary powers. They also clarify the duties implicit in the fiduciary relationship.

Prudent Man Rule

This is usually defined as the duty of a fiduciary to exercise the same degree of skill and care that a person of ordinary prudence exercises in the management of his or her own property and affairs. It is also applied to all of a bank's acts performed in servicing all of its customers, whether in an agency or fiduciary capacity.

It is not too difficult to imagine how this requirement can be applied to almost any administrative act throughout the life of a trust, from the investment of trust funds through the distribution of income and ultimately of the corpus of the trust.

Where corporate fiduciaries are concerned, however, the courts are very likely to demand a higher degree of skill and care than they would from the individual or nonprofessional trustee. The reasoning behind this attitude is sound and easy to understand. Banks and trust companies are professional fiduciaries who present themselves to the public as experts of unquestionable reliability and integrity. The courts therefore feel that in the interest of maintaining the public's confidence, they should be held to a higher degree of care and skill.

Duty of Undivided Loyalty

This duty is the heart, the very essence of the fiduciary relationship and requires the trustee and executor to administer the trust and estate for the sole benefit of the beneficiaries. Fiduciaries may not profit in any way from their uniquely advantageous position. Neither may they engage in any transaction or undertaking that might prevent them from exercising their best judgment on behalf of the estate or trust, or adversely affect the interests of the beneficiaries or other interested parties.

Duty To Carry Out Administration

A trustee or executor may not renegue on its agreement to undertake the administration of a trust or estate, no matter how burdensome or unprofitable the undertaking might be. It may, of course, petition the court of jurisdiction and/or the beneficiaries or other interested parties for permission to resign.

Duty Not To Delegate

Fiduciaries are required to perform those duties expected of them, specifically those involving the exercise of discretion, wisdom, judgment, and specialized skills. Fiduciaries commit a breach of trust when they permit others to do these things for them. They may, of course, employ agents to take care of routine matters that do not involve the exercise of discretion, wisdom, judgment, or specialized skills.

Duty To Protect and Conserve Property, Both Real and Personal, That Has Been Entrusted to Them

Loss of property or a decline in its value results, eventually, in the reduction or loss of income to the beneficiaries. The distributees of an estate or the remaindermen of a trust will also suffer. A fiduciary must protect everyone's interest.

Duty To Make Trust Income-Producing

Trustees

Most governing instruments grant investment control to the trustee, or to the trustee and a co-trustee jointly. Each one is individually liable for the prompt and prudent investment of the principal or corpus of the trust to produce a maximum of income for the beneficiaries.

Executors and Administrators

The investment of estate funds is normally not one of the duties of executors or administrators. Their duties with respect to estate assets are, properly, conservation and prompt distribution to the legatees, distributees, and trustees. There are, however, many instances when cash is being held for taxes, distribution, and expenses, and, depending on the circumstances, it might be prudent for the executor or administrator to make careful, temporary, short-term investments (for example, in treasury bills, certificates of deposit, or savings accounts) until the funds are needed.

Duty To Maintain Account Records and Render Accountings

This is a rather basic and obvious duty but one that is not always performed in a satisfactory manner. Separate accounts must be maintained for income and principal. Executors and trustees must be able to show from their records what they originally received, what they paid out, what gains or losses occurred, what income was collected, and, among other items, how much they took in fees. Fiduciaries must also comply with requests from beneficiaries, remaindermen, and courts of jurisdiction for information and for an accounting of their administration of the estate or trust. Failure to keep accurate and complete records and the resulting inability to provide satisfactory information usually result in a ruling by the courts against the fiduciary.

Duty To Take and Maintain Control of Estate and Trust Property

Executors and trustees are under a duty to take physical possession of all estate and trust assets, including the enforcement of all of the estate's or trust's claims against third parties. The fiduciary must continue to retain physical possession in a safe and tightly controlled manner. Estate and trust assets should not be allowed to remain in the possession of others, except of course in such obvious situations as the sale, exchange, or collection of securities or where real estate or similar property is involved. In the latter case, the fiduciary must make certain that the property is recorded in the name of the estate or trust.

Duty To Keep Estate and Trust Property Separate and Apart from the Personal Property of the Fiduciary and from the Property of Other Estates and Trusts

A fiduciary many not mingle estate or trust assets with his own or with those of other estates or trusts, except where the fiduciary is permitted by the terms of the governing instrument to hold the assets of related trusts "in solido" for ease of administration, or where participation in a common trust fund maintained by the corporate trustee is permitted.

In some jurisdictions, New York being one of them, there has for some time been a trend to physically consolidate the assets of employee benefit trusts and depend on the account records and assets controls for identification of each trust's portion of each issue.

Duty To Identify Trust Property

A fiduciary may not register estate or trust property in its own name. The property must be registered in the fiduciary's name as executor or trustee, or in the name of a corporate trustee's nominee where it is permitted by the governing instrument and/or applicable statutory law.

Duty To Remit Income to Beneficiaries

A trustee must remit income promptly to the beneficiary, either as required by the governing instrument or within a reasonable time after it has been received. It is not reasonable to expect a fiduciary to remit income as soon as it has been received, because time is required to compute commissions, pay expenses, and so forth. (The income due beneficiaries is net income, not gross.) However, if the fiduciary takes too long to remit income, the fiduciary is liable for interest due.

Duty To Treat Beneficiaries Impartially

Where a trust has more than one beneficiary, the trustee must treat them equitably unless there is a provision to the contrary. Sometimes the trust instrument gives the trustee the power to exercise discretion in the distribution of income among several beneficiaries. Under such circumstances, the trustee must be objective and use good judgment. The trustee must not be influenced by personal feelings or the feelings of others.

Responsibility of Co-Trustees

Where there are two or more trustees, each trustee is equally responsible for the administration of the trust. The exercise of discretionary power must be approved by each trustee unless the will or trust agreement provides otherwise. One trustee may not delegate his discretionary duties to another. If one trustee acts improperly, the other(s) will be equally liable if they do not force the offending fiduciary to take corrective action.

It is not difficult, after considering the ramifications of the foregoing, to imagine how easy it is for a fiduciary to run into trouble. The feeling of "living on the razor's edge" is always present. Equitable administration of a trust involves sensitive and often delicate balancing of the equities of a particular situation, rather than deciding by a formula or by rule of thumb. It is the dispensation of justice of a very high order for a particular set of facts and circumstances that cannot always be anticipated in advance. Each situation must be judged on its own merits, in the light of conditions existing at the time and in accordance with law and fiduciary principles.

A fiduciary incurs liability by acting imperfectly, by acting improperly, and by failing to act when necessary. In legal parlance, these conditions are sometimes referred to as misfeasance, malfeasance, and nonfeasance, and are brought about by the exercise or nonexercise of fiduciary duties and powers, express, discretionary, and implied.

Other Personal Fiduciary Services

Guardianships

A guardian is an individual or professional fiduciary appointed by a court of jurisdiction to care for either the property or person of a minor, or both. In either case, the guardian is accountable to the court of jurisdiction for the administration of the property and the person.

Committeeship

A committee has duties similar to those of a guardian, but is normally involved in connection with an incompetent. The committee is also closely supervised by the courts of jurisdiction.

Employee Benefit Trusts

Although employee benefit trusts are comparatively recent arrivals on the fiduciary scene, especially when one considers the truly ancient origins of personal trusts, they have nevertheless experienced a spectacularly rapid growth during the past thirty years. Employee benefit trusts existed many years before the early thirties, but not in any great number. Moreover, the plans were for the most part voluntary, informal, and an expression of sincere charitable concern on the part of employers for their retiring employees.

There were no guarantees that the funds would survive or that there would be any intervention by the government in the event that the trusts did become insolvent. Many factors have contributed to the rapid growth of these trusts: inflation, which has been creeping up on us since World War I; federal tax exemptions for contributions made by employers; the need on the part of employers in an expanding economy to attract and retain desirable personnel; union activity; and the very real concern of employers for the welfare of their people.

The asset value of public and private employee benefit trusts, which are managed by banks and life insurance companies, is over $200 billion. This staggering value has attracted the close attention of legislative and investigating committees of both state and federal governments. To qualify for tax exemption, these plans must meet the requirements set forth in the Internal Revenue Code. Until passage of the Employee Retirement Income Security Act of 1974, this code for all practical purposes determined not only the provisions of the plan and trust agreement, but also the future acts of the company and the trustee. The Employee Retirement Income Security Act, or ERISA, as it is more familiarly known, imposes even more stringent requirements than those originally set forth in the Internal Revenue Code. Both the plan and reporting requirements are so complex that the corporation and the trustee must have high-powered, expert advice and support to be sure they are not in violation of any of the provisions of ERISA or the Internal Revenue Code. Thus legal, tax, and actuarial advice is an enormous expense factor in the establishment and administration of qualified employee benefit trusts.

Although there is a world of difference between personal and employee benefit trusts, and although the liability of the trustee is deliberately restricted by the trust agreement, the trustee is still required to exercise the same degree of care and to demonstrate the same fidelity to the trust that is required of it as trustee of a personal trust. Further, because it publicly represents itself as an expert, and in spite of any exculpatory provisions in the agreement, it must guard against participating with the company in acts that might adversely affect the interests of the beneficiaries. It must go on record as being opposed to such acts, and even, in certain instances, ask to resign.

There are several types of employee benefit trust.

Pension Trusts

A pension trust is based on a plan designed to pay retiring employees a specified pension for their remaining years. The amount is arrived at by a formula involving the employee's salary, the corporation's ability to contribute, and other factors such as the cost of living and the projected rate of return on the funds to be invested. The plan is designed with the help of counsel, a qualified actuary, and the selected trustee. It must comply with the provisions of the Internal Revenue Code, ERISA, national and state banking requirements, the Federal Deposit Insurance Corporation, and the State Insurance Department. A pension plan may be contributory or noncontributory, that is, the employee may be required to make monthly contributions or the employer may assume the entire contribution.

Profit-Sharing Trusts

Profit-sharing trusts, like pension trusts, are established in accordance with a plan and administered by a trustee under the provisions of a trust agreement. To be a qualified plan, that is, to have contributions by the employer tax deductible as in the case of a qualified pension plan, it must also comply with the provisions of the Internal Revenue Code and ERISA. The employer normally establishes such a trust to enable the employee to share in the profits of the business.

The employer may also use it as a retirement plan, but the amount the employee receives at retirement is not predetermined as under a pension plan. Rather, it depends entirely on the profits earned and contributed by the company, and on the return from the investments in which they were placed. Profit-sharing trusts usually are set up in addition to a pension trust, in which case the employee may either withdraw set percentages periodically or allow the money to remain until retirement or termination of employment for other reasons.

Savings Incentive Plans

A savings incentive plan is primarily a way to provide supplementary pension benefits by making it possible for employees to use their savings, together with their employers' matching contributions, to enhance their ultimate retirement benefits. Whatever the employee elects to set aside, in keeping with the plan's requirements, is matched by the employer, in some instances by as much as two hundred percent of the employee's contribution. This money is then invested, again in keeping with the provisions of the plan, in any one or more of the investment options provided for in the plan.

There are other employee benefit plans such as Stock Ownership Plans, Self Employed Retirement Trusts, and Individual Retirement Accounts. A Stock Ownership Plan is a plan offered by employers to reward employees for exceptional service by providing for bonuses in the form of company stock. Here again, there must be compliance with the requirements of the Internal Revenue Code and ERISA.

Self Employed Retirement Trusts, or H.R. 10-Keogh Plans, and Individual Retirement Accounts enable those not covered by any other pension plan to enjoy, to a degree, the same benefits accorded employees of corporations that have established qualified pension and/or profit-sharing trusts.

Corporate Trusts

It has been previously stated that commercial enterprises use short-term loans to finance their seasonal needs for working capital, and that as soon as their new inventory is sold off, part of the proceeds is used to pay off the loan. Sometimes their need for fixed asset financing, such as financing for plants and equipment, results in term loans, or loans to be repaid periodically over approximately a year. There are, however, times when the commercial borrower may need very large sums of money and require several years to pay back the loan. The usual commercial lending mechanism probably could not accommodate a loan of this proportion, nor would it want to do so. The corporation must, therefore, look to the investing public for funds.

In a situation such as this, the potential corporate borrower can take advantage of the trust indenture, a unique tool that facilitates this type of borrowing. The trust indenture enables the borrower to go to individual investors and induce them to invest their funds in the corporation's bonds without having to negotiate hundreds of thousands of individual loan agreements. It is the trust indenture, or trust agreement, that must conform to the provisions of the Trust Indenture Act of 1939. This act is in effect an appendage of the Securities Exchange Acts of 1933 and 1934, whose sole purpose was to protect the investing public that had suffered tremendous losses because of the lack of government regulation. The Trust Indenture Act of 1939 set forth very stringent requirements for corporations wishing to issue debt securities. A trustee had to be selected and an agreement drawn up between the issuer and the trustee, whose primary function was to protect the interests of the investing public. This act is still in effect today, and the trust indenture must conform in every detail to the statutory requirements. The trustee also protects the corporation wishing to issue the bonds by monitoring its compliance with the provisions of the agreement and with applicable regulations. The trust indenture is a very complex and highly technical instrument, and before it reaches the signing stage, counsel for both the corporation and the trustee must review its provisions very carefully.

In contrast to personal and employee benefit trust agreements, under this type of agreement the trustee has no legal ownership in any property that might have been pledged to secure the corporate debt, unless the corporation defaults on its obligation. The same fiduciary principles of fidelity to trust and so forth still apply, but it is obvious that this type of trustee cannot interfere in the management of the corporation, nor is it privy to the inside philosophy and plans of the corporation's management. Often the trustee must make decisions, sometimes far reaching, without being able to secure agreement from the holders of the debt securities.

The most important duty of the corporate trustee is to ensure compliance with the provisions of the trust indenture under which the bonds were sold to the investing public. If the corporation should default on its obligations, the trustee is the most important protector of the investor. The trustee must make certain that all of the protective or remedial measures provided in the trust indenture and by law are observed and enforced.

It is logical and practical that the corporate trustee also be appointed by the issuing corporation to perform those routine but critical bookkeeping and financial duties related to servicing the debt. For example, the trustee may serve in the capacity of a registrar, paying agent, exchange agent, transfer agent, or dividend disbursing agent.

Registrar

The registrar maintains an up-to-date record of all registered holders of the outstanding bonds. It should be noted, however, that not all bondholders are registered. Many hold bonds that are in bearer form, that is, not registered in the name of the holder, and have semi-annual interest coupons attached. Bearer bonds are negotiable bonds and normally may be sold without any red tape. The bearer is deemed to be the owner, and interest in the form of coupon redemption is routine.

Paying Agent

Principal

When bonds reach maturity, the corporation needs someone to pay the holders when they present the bonds for redemption. Very often it is practical to appoint the trustee to take care of this, although sometimes co-agents are appointed to take care of those holders who may be geographically scattered. In addition, if the trust indenture has sinking fund provisions, bonds may be called for redemption prior to the maturity date recorded on the face of the bond.

Income

Holders of bearer bonds clip the semi-annual interest coupons attached to the bond certificates and send them in for collection through their own banks, who in turn send them to the interest-paying agent for that corporation.

Registered bond holders, on the other hand, do not have to take any action to collect the interest due on their bonds. In this case, the paying agent is the registrar and interest checks are routinely sent out to holders of record.

Exchange Agent

The trustee must validate all new bonds issued. Thus the corporate trustee performs an important service when bearer bonds are presented for exchange into registered bonds, or vice versa, or when bonds are presented for exchange into different denominations.

Transfer Agent

The words "transfer agent" are usually associated with the transfer of stock from one owner to another, but transfers also occur with bonds. However, in the case of bonds, the transfer agent is usually called the "registrar." A stock transfer agent is concerned with compliance with state and federal laws and regulations, including taxes due on the transactions. The transfer agent is also responsible for verifying that there has been no quantity of shares of stock issued in excess of the amount authorized by the issuer's charter or articles of incorporation. In addition, the transfer agent must determine the right of a holder to transfer the stock into his or her own name, which becomes particularly technical and involved when shares are held in the name of a trust, estate, or fiduciary. Certified copies of wills, trust agreements, letters testamentary, or letters of administration, and other documents are usually required by the transfer agent. These are known as legal transfers and take an inordinate amount of time to complete. For this reason, corporate fiduciaries usually have trust and estate securities as well as securities held in custodian accounts registered in the name of one or more of their own nominees where state law permits it and if there is no provision in the governing instrument prohibiting it. The use of a nominee, which is a legal partnership composed of one or more officials of the bank into whose name fiduciary and custodian securities are transferred, eliminates most of the legal red tape involved in the transfer of securities and also facilitates the collection of dividends and interest. Instead of having to collect thousands of dividend checks for a particular stock held in thosands of individual accounts, the dividend agent sends perhaps three or four checks of very large amounts for all of the shares, which the bank subsequently allocates among the accounts involved.

Dividend Disbursing Agent

Since transfer agents maintain stockholder records for corporations, they are normally dividend disbursing agents for those corporations.

SECURITIES PROCESSING SERVICES

This function is in reality a clearing service for securities transactions, such as purchases and sales, redemptions, and exchanges, that are initiated by the bank's investment portfolio management, its personal and employee benefit trust departments, its custodian customers, and all other customers, including correspondent banks, nonbanking corporations, savings banks, noncorporate business enterprises, government agencies, universities, hospitals, endowment funds, churches and individuals, all of whom could also be custodian customers. Banks specializing in this service are located in cities where major stock exchanges are located. New York City is the center of the securities industry. The New York Stock Exchange, the American Stock Exchange, and the Over-The-Counter Securities Market, are all located in New York, which is also the center of transfer and registrar services. Some other centers of securities activity are Chicago, San Francisco, and Boston.

Nature of the Services

After receiving valid instructions from its customers, the trust and custodian departments, the securities clearing operation will, on the normal delivery date, also known as the settlement date, perform the following services.

1   It will receive or accept securities purchased, examine and count them, verify their negotiability, and pay for

them; collect any dividends due on stock purchases, have the certificates transferred in accordance with instructions, and, upon return from the transfer agent, ship them to the customer, ship them to a third party, if so instructed, or deposit them in the proper trust or custodian accounts in the vault or in the bank's own investment portfolio. It will also pass through the charges to the proper accounts for the cost of the securities purchased.

2 It will receive securities "free" of payment, examine them, count them, verify their negotiability, have them transferred as per instructions, and, upon return from the transfer agent, dispose of them as instructed. "Free" securities could include estate and trust assets being delivered to the trust department, dividends in shares of the stock of the issuing corporation, stock splits, and so forth.

3 It will deliver out on the settlement date securities sold against receipt of proceeds, or securities being redeemed against receipt of proceeds, and credit the proper accounts with these proceeds.

4 It will deliver, "free" of payment, securities to remaindermen of terminating trusts and distributees or legatees of estates, and stock certificates received as dividends to beneficiaries of trusts or to other customers or third parties as gifts.

This is a very broad description of a very complicated and vital service, and it in no way indicates the tremendous amount of control and accounting work involved. The interdepartmental accounting, processing, and control systems involved form a most intricate network, to say nothing of the processing, accounting, and control systems among the banks, brokers, and several securities clearing agencies on "the street". In recent years, very sophisticated, on-line, real-time automated systems have been developed and implemented by banks, brokers, stock exchanges, and their clearing agencies, but the securities industry still remains a very labor-intensive industry, primarily because of the ever-present need to physically process securities certificates.

Depository Trust Company

In the bull market of the late 1960s and early 1970s, the securities industry was brought to its knees by an unprecedented volume of trading that broke the back of a collection of manual, antiquated, and inadequate securities processing systems. Banks, brokers, and the stock exchanges were to blame for not having paid enough attention to their back offices over the years. The situation was so catastrophic that brokers had to close early and sometimes not even open in order to stem the tide of transactions and attendant paper work that was engulfing them. Banks were forced to call a moratorium on new business because they could not handle it. Unmatched trades, "don't know" deliveries, duplicate deliveries, staggering accounts receivables, and funds held awaiting payment proved too much for the banks to handle. Consultants from all over converged on "the street," and the consensus of opinion was that automation and, above all, immobilization of the stock and bond certificates were imperative and immediate priorities. The history of this monumental effort is too mind boggling to go into, but out of it all emerged the driving force on "the street," the Banking and Securities Industry Committee (BASIC). The members of this committee were a group of high-powered, top banking and stock exchange executives who, because of impending disaster and the threat of government intervention and regulation, literally forced both sides of the industry to work together and give birth to the Depository Trust Company (DTC). DTC began as a child of the Stock Clearing Corporation, a wholly owned subsidiary of the New York Stock Exchange, and grew into a giant of a book-entry system and depository for banks and brokers.

DTC is a limited-purpose, nonprofit trust company chartered by the New York State Banking Board on February 27, 1973. On April 23 of the same year it became a member of the Federal Reserve System. It is owned and managed by the banks and brokers and is under the supervision of the banking and securities industry regulatory bodies. Participating banks deposit their trust and other customers' securities with DTC, which cancels them and sets up on-line computer, book-entry records of the banks' deposits. Trades can then be completed between the banks and the brokers, who have also deposited large inventories of securities with DTC, through bookkeeping entries, thus eliminating physical deliveries and their attendant time-consuming and error-prone processing steps. It also affords protection against loss caused by negligence or theft.

Other regional depositories soon followed suit, and at the present time there is a Midwest Depository, a Pacific Depository, a New England Depository, and a Philadelphia Depository. There is close computer communication among all the depositories with regard to trades executed by participants and their customers on the different exchanges. Because of their nonprofit status, they also offer a wide range of securities services at nominal cost; this is particularly true of the Depository Trust Company in New York. This does not especially please participating banks, who market the same services at a much higher price. To a degree, the depositories are in competition with the banks, although many customers prefer to participate in a depository through their correspondent banks, which provide them with a buffer and protection by virtue of their sophisticated accounting and control systems and their written guarantees of protection against loss.

Federal Reserve Book-Entry System

This is comparable to DTC except that it is exclusively devoted to U.S. government and agency securities. However, DTC, which is a member of the Federal Reserve System, can settle government trades for its participants because it can interface with the Federal Reserve Book-Entry System.

BANK VAULT SERVICES

The bank vault houses securities held for trust department accounts, custodian accounts, and the bank's own investment portfolio. It also houses securities held as collateral for commercial loans and investment bankers' and brokers' loans, securities held pending completion of processing, securities and other items of value from the general cage pending completion of processing, last-minute items received by the trust and custodian departments for processing the next morning, and of course the tellers' cash, including the reserve cash. Except for securities held in trust department accounts, custodian accounts, and the bank's own investment portfolio, all other securities and items of value, including collateral, are under the control of the departments, divisions, and other areas housing them in the vault overnight. These latter-designated areas place them in the vault in locked or sealed containers overnight and take them out the next business day.

Vault management and control are highly sensitive and responsible duties; those in charge should not report to any area that deposits securities or items of value in the vault. Vault officers are in a way, comparable to auditing officers in that they should be independent of interference and intimidation by those who use their service and should be free to faithfully adhere to prescribed operating and control procedures. There should be a vault committee composed of officers of departments that do not use the vault and, of course, the auditor. Operating and control procedures should be in writing and distributed to those who use the vault as well as to all vault personnel.

SAFE DEPOSIT SERVICES

Many bankers have said it is a source of wonder that any bank offers safe deposit services because of the liability involved. Safe deposit customers rent boxes for an annual fee that is, considering the liability, rather nominal. The return on this service is marginal, considering the controls and precautionary measures that should be observed, although it is a known fact that they are not always observed. The rental of safe deposit boxes really is in the nature of a public service.

Procedures Involved

1 Access to the box involves two people, the lessee, who has a key for one-half the combination, and the vault officer, whose key opens the other half.
2 Access should not be granted to anyone who is not authorized to enter the box, and signatures should be verified.
3 Date and time of entry and departure should be recorded by the vault attendant.
4 The vault attendant should show the lessee or his or her deputy into a customer's private room where he or she can examine, deposit, or remove part or all of the contents. This is a private matter and the vault attendant has no right to know what is in the box.

There are many other details involving who the lessee is; for example, a private individual, a corporation or partnership, or a church. However, the outstanding liability confronting every banker is that the bank, in the event of a loss claimed by the lessee, cannot prove definitively that the lessee did not own the claimed missing items or did not place them in the box. This potential liability becomes even more distressing when the boxes are burglarized and all of the contents stolen.

INTERNATIONAL BANKING

The objectives of a bank's international banking department are basically not very different from those of its domestic banking department, except that other critical considerations come into play. A bank is dealing with customers whose banking and business practices differ from American banking and business practices, whose attitudes and mores are, in most instances, quite different, and whose various cultural backgrounds and outlooks affect their dealings with other countries. Political conditions in each country vary and must be taken into consideration. Language problems are no small matter, either.

In spite of these obstacles, an international banking department of an American bank is interested in promoting international trade by lending to and servicing foreign corporations abroad, lending to and servicing foreign subsidiaries of American corporations abroad, lending to and servicing American subsidiaries of foreign corporations, and lending to and providing personal service to foreign nationals here and abroad. The international banking department facilitates these loans and services by maintaining deposits in banks in foreign countries, accepting deposits from foreign banks and corporations here in the United States, issuing and accepting commercial and travelers' letters of credit and bankers' acceptances, and providing other necessary services such as transfers of funds, supplies of foreign currencies, and air freight.

American banks usually operate out of branch or representative offices in foreign countries and through a large and knowledgable foreign correspondent bank in each country. This is vitally important in order to keep in touch with financial and political developments abroad.

Foreign Exchange Function

Foreign exchange involves the buying and selling of foreign currencies on any foreign currency market throughout the world. The prices paid are computed in terms of the currency of the country in which the buying or selling is initiated, that is, how much it costs in terms of U.S. dollars. It is a very volatile business, and demands a very keen knowledge of foreign exchange markets in different parts of the world.

Importers and exporters are the primary customers of this division and depend upon it to get the very best rates available. If the currency is needed for immediate shipment, the purchase is called a "spot" transaction, but if it won't be needed for, say, 60 to 90 days, the trader will enter into a future contract that hopefully will protect the buyer against future upward fluctuations in price by fixing his price at the time of the contract. The reverse also is true for a seller. It is quite obvious that trading in foreign currencies is a risky business and requires the acumen, knowledge, and experience of a seasoned trader.

Letters of Credit

The instrument known as a letter of credit was developed and refined over the years as a means of facilitating the purchase and sale of merchandise internationally. For example, a manufacturing firm based in the United States might have a customer in Spain. The firm will want to make certain that the customer won't cancel the order after work has begun on it, that the firm won't have to wait months for its money, and that, in fact, it will be paid. It is often very difficult to determine the credit standing of foreign customers or to understand their business customs and practices. The exporter therefore will ask the foreign customer to arrange for the customer's bank to provide a commercial letter of credit. The bank the customer selects is also a matter of concern to the selling firm and to its bank, which will be asked to confirm the letter of credit.

When the seller is a foreign firm and the importer is an American firm, the situation is reversed and the latter must arrange for a letter of credit with its bank to be sent to the bank of the foreign exporter.

Among the various types of letters of credit, two are of prime significance, the revocable and the irrevocable letter of credit. Since the former can be cancelled or amended at any time without advice to or consent of either the seller or his bank, it offers very little protection and is rarely used. The irrevocable instrument cannot be cancelled or amended without the consent of the seller and the confirming bank. Each letter of credit is a unique agreement unto itself and must be studied in detail. Generalizations in this business are dangerous and nothing should be assumed. It is an agreement custom-tailored to suit the wishes of the seller.

The bank that issues a letter of credit agrees to pay the selling firm if it has complied with all the conditions set forth. It sends the letter of credit to the advising and confirming bank in the seller's country; the bank then advises the seller that it has received a letter of credit in the seller's favor. When the selling firm is ready to ship the merchandise, it presents all the required documents, including the draft to the confirming bank, which either pays the seller immediately if it is a "sight" draft, or agrees to pay at maturity if it is a "time" draft. Everything depends on the conditions in the letter of agreement. In any event, all the documents are forwarded to the issuing bank for reimbursement to the confirming bank.

RESOURCES MANAGEMENT

The successful management of a bank's resources, or the safe and profitable investment of its deposits and other funds, is the primary responsibility of top management. It requires financial skill of the highest order, particularly in today's economic environment. A bank's earning asset mix—that is, its commercial loans, installment loans, investment securities, trading securities, real estate loans, interest-bearing deposits with other banks, federal funds sold, and securities purchased under resale agreements —reflects the quality of management's financial know-how and ability to anticipate money market trends and its own short- and long-term needs. A bank's investments are always the target of regulatory examiners' and certified public accountants' intense scrutiny and analysis.

Investment Securities

A bank's investment securities are not only interest-earning assets. They also constitute that part of the earning asset mix that represents a bank's liquidity, or its ability to make funds readily available for loans or other purposes. This requires careful planning in selecting maturities, in evaluating the credit quality of securities, in selecting types of securities, and in determining their effective yields. It should be noted that commercial banks are not permitted by law to buy stocks for their own portfolios. (There are certain relatively unimportant exceptions to this prohibition, but they have no significance to this discussion.) The responsibility for managing the securities portfolio should be assigned to a special committee appointed by the board. This committee should make certain that the policy, strategy, and decisions on buying and selling are in writing and available to those who must carry out these decisions. All transactions should be reviewed, ultimately, by the board.

In addition, efficient systems for securities processing, control, accounting, and safekeeping are mandatory and should be reviewed periodically.

It has been stated that the purpose of this book is not to make auditors of its readers. That would be unlikely, if not impossible. Its purpose is to acquaint the interested reader with the need for internal auditing, the objectives of internal auditing, the techniques that might be employed, and, of equal importance, to make the reader realize the scope and depth of knowledge an internal auditor must have of the banking industry or any other industry before having the temerity to launch an auditing program. Supported by sufficient knowledge, internal auditing can be an adventure.

It should be apparent even to the most casual reader that it is not feasible within the constraints of this book to touch upon all the facets of all of the banking functions. For each banking function and service there are underlying, complex systems of processing, accounting, and control that would take at least two volumes to explain; even then, the explanation would probably be found wanting. Many functions, such as check processing, the transit operation, purchasing, general services, mortgages, and real estate have not been mentioned because it did not seem necessary to bring the point across. Perhaps too much detail has been given in some areas and too little in others. Reaction will depend upon the reader's background. If a reader has a good background in banking and in auditing, that reader will probably appreciate the magnitude of the auditing effort. On the other hand, those who are knowledgeable may find this discussion inadequate for their purposes; those who are not, may have expected more. Hopefully, most of the readers have been reached.

4

Approaches to the Internal Bank Audit Function

Conceptually, the internal bank audit function is simple and straightforward. Its success, though, depends heavily on:

1 The auditor's knowledge of the bank, its organization, its functions and services, and their underlying accounting, processing, and control systems;
2 The adequacy and competency of the entire auditing staff.
3 The strategic organization of that staff.
4 The auditor's knowledge of applicable banking law and regulations.

Auditors must also be aware of the areas most susceptible to error and fraud in each function as well as in their supporting systems. If auditors are not alert to these sensitivities, their audits and tests will not be focused specifically on these areas, and error patterns and fraud might not be uncovered. Any existing error and fraud will then continue until it is too late to prevent losses.

The problem is that the only way auditors can become aware of the sensitive areas is to learn the hard way, by delving into the bank's systems and procedures and finding out how they work. Ideally, the auditor must be thoroughly knowledgable about every area of a bank. Because this is not possible in large banks, however, teams of specialists must be formed. The chief auditor of course must be a well-informed, strong generalist.

There is a current and much discussed case that will be, or should be, referred to in the annals of auditing history as a classic example of the violations of basic elementary controls and, equally important, as an outstanding example of the auditor's apparent failure to have correctly analyzed and evaluated an operating system and its component procedures. This is the "Wells Fargo Bank Case," which will be discussed in more detail later. Briefly, the bank was the victim of an embezzlement resulting in a loss of $21,300,000, not a small sum. It is, of course, entirely possible that the auditor did correctly identify the weaknesses of the system and procedures, but that no one wanted to pay any attention. This unfortunately does happen. It is also possible that management might be to blame for not having provided an adequate auditing staff, and that the areas involved were on the auditor's agenda of things to do when people could be released to do them. It has been referred to by the press as a combination of "computers and volume," which is really not an entirely accurate description.

The establishment of an effectively structured internal auditing program for an entire bank is a far from easy task. Being responsible for the safety of all operations is, as has been illustrated, a formidable undertaking. What is the best approach or combination of approaches? Should every customer transaction and every general ledger account be audited in detail for accuracy and validity? If not, why not? Why would it be neither feasible nor desirable? What other valid and viable options does an auditor have to make certain that each transaction has every chance of being safely and accurately processed, that conditions conducive to error and fraud are reduced to a minimum, and that approved policies and procedures as well as applicable laws and regulations are receiving compliance?

Continuous Auditing

This is usually one of the answers of an uninformed and panicky management. In a flurry of fear, their answer is to review each transaction, every day. The recomputation and/or validation of every transaction and the review of every account is definitely not a satisfactory answer. It is, in the long run, totally unworkable and most ineffective. The maintenance of duplicate records is even worse, as is the installation of resident auditors in every critical area. In addition, continuous auditing is totally unproductive and destructive because it usurps the duties and powers of operating management, who are being paid to make the operations safe and efficient.

Auditing should not become a substitute for required operating, accounting, and other internal controls. If auditing is permitted to become a substitute, a bank's operations are weakened because its management will tend to rely on auditing instead of installing and enforcing the necessary controls. This will lead to disaster. The auditor's job is not to interfere or exercise control, but to see that all banking operations are efficient and effectively controlled independently of the auditing function.

If the auditor becomes totally involved in finding and correcting errors, the audit function is reduced to a fire-fighting operation. The auditor has no time to find out why errors are occurring, and therefore is in no position to develop and recommend corrective and preventive measures. In other words, the auditor is treating the symptoms instead of curing the disease. Under these conditions, auditing also tends to become mechanical and self-defeating. The monotony of the repetitive activity causes the auditor to see what should be there rather than what actually is recorded. This is common knowledge. Almost everyone has heard auditors and management wonder out loud why so obvious an error or departure from approved operating procedure was not discovered sooner.

Auditing of this type is very costly not only because of duplication of effort, but also because as volume increases, more auditors must be employed. This increase in the auditing staff is soon brought to an abrupt end because the cost cannot be justified by a measurable return; even under ideal circumstances, this is the nemesis of the auditing profession. Finally and most importantly, continuous auditing is an impossibility in large- and medium-sized banks, where management could never justify the cost of enough auditors to cover every transaction on an ongoing basis.

There are, however, certain situations in which this approach might be justified and perhaps workable. In very small banks where recommended internal controls cannot be implemented because the cost of staffing would be prohibitive, continuous auditing might be the only answer. Under extenuating circumstances, as in the case of suspected fraud or embezzlement, it might be necessary on a temporary basis. It might also be used for special purpose accounts requiring constant vigilance because they are extremely critical and susceptible to fraud, embezzlement, and erorr.

EXAMINATIONS

Examinations differ from other internal audits and reviews in that as of a given date, all accounting, processing, control, and other details of a department or of the entire bank are examined and proved to general ledger account controls. Particular attention is given to compliance with bank policies, approved operating procedures, and applicable statutory laws and regulations. Examinations can be very effective if they are carefully planned and meticulously carried out and if they include sending requests for confirmation to customers, clearing banks, agents holding securities (for transfer, redemption, and so forth), and other banks where the bank has funds on deposit. They reassure management that all was in order and accounted for as of the date of the examination. It must be remembered, though, that the very next day anything could go wrong. That is why ongoing internal auditing is so very important.

Annual Directors' Examinations

These examinations are performed to comply with statutory requirements such as state banking laws, in the case of state-chartered banks, or the Regulations of the Comptroller of the Currency, in the case of nationally chartered banks.

These examinations are not usually performed by the directors, nor are they expected to be. Rather, they are ordered by the directors and carried out by the internal auditing staff or by outside certified public accountants hired by the directors. In some respects, Directors' Examinations are rather antiquated requirements, particularly in those banks that have well-staffed auditing departments and adequate internal auditing programs.

There are other reasons that contribute to the argument against Directors' Examinations. First, most bank directors are inexperienced and unfamiliar with many of the functions and operations of the bank, and therefore could not conduct an examination of any value by themselves. They are nevertheless responsible for the safety and financial stability of the bank, which is why they should have a well-staffed and professional internal auditing department reporting to a directors' examining and audit committee. This committee normally employs a firm of well-known certified public accountants to review the program and the work of the internal auditing department. Second, Directors' Examinations are expected to cover the entire bank. It is therefore not reasonable to believe that they would provide much more than lip service to the statutory requirements, particularly in large commercial banks. And last, where large commercial banks with many branches are concerned, such examinations have been reduced by banking regulatory authorities in many states to simply an official certification of a statement of condition as of the date of the examination, with express reliance on an internal auditing program to support this certification.

The requirement for an annual Directors' Examination is not entirely unjustified, though, because there are banks that prefer not to spend much, if any, money on an internal auditing program. However, Directors' Examinations should not be substituted for an internal auditing program because the internal auditing program is a continuing function whose objective is the prevention and detection of loss caused by fraud and negligence. Fraud and negligence are continuing realities that do not freeze at any given point in time. The Directors' Examination was not intended to be a substitute for a good internal auditing program.

Many of the techniques employed in directors' examinations are also used by the internal bank auditor conducting periodic examinations of individual departments. An effective examination of an entire bank as of a given date is virtually an impossibility unless the bank is very small.

Some of the concerns of a Directors' Examination are the following:

1 Physical verification of a bank's assets to proven accounting records and their proof to the general ledger controls.
2 Verification of the bank's liabilities and capital accounts, that is, deposits, outstanding stock, and indebtedness to the general ledger controls.
3 A determination that there has been compliance with official policies and approved procedures, particularly with respect to commercial loans and investment securities.
4 A determination that there has been no violation of applicable statutory laws and regulations.
5 A determination that an evaluation of the quality of performance has been made of both operating and administrative management.

Internal Auditing Examinations of Specific Functions and Departments

These examinations should be part of a carefully planned internal auditing program. Their frequency will depend on the relative importance of the function involved, its vulnerability to theft of items of value, and its susceptibility to fraud and error.

Objectives

These examinations have a number of objectives.

1 To make certain that as of a given date, all items of value are physically accounted for. These include such items as securities held in safekeeping, collateral held to secure loans, cash held in the tellers' positions and in vault reserves, securities held by transfer agents, securities held over in the course of processing, unissued government bonds, unissued letters of credit, unissued official checks, and many other similar items that represent potential value.

2 To determine that departmental or divisional records are accurate, agree with general ledger controls, and correctly reflect the transactions processed that day.

3 To make certain that approved systems and procedures are being followed and continue to be adequate.

4 To determine that established systems of control are receiving compliance and continue to be effective.

5 To make certain that there have been no violations of official policy or applicable laws and regulations.

Procedures

Examinations should be well planned in advance. Auditors should be briefed, have written instructions, know the function well, and have reviewed the reports of previous examinations. As much as possible, there should be no advance warning of the impending examination. The element of surprise in all audits is invaluable.

1   Cash, securities held in safekeeping, securities held as collateral for loans, securities held over in the course of processing, and all other items of value or potential value should be examined, counted, and proved to departmental subsidiary control records and, where applicable, to the bank's general ledger controls. Securities held in safekeeping for custodian or trust account customers cannot be part of a bank's general ledger because they are not assets of the bank. Only securities held in the bank's own investment account are recorded on the bank's general ledger.

2   All subsidiary departmental accounting controls should be run, proved to their respective general ledger accounts, and reviewed for validity and aging of items, such as accounts receivable and funds held awaiting payment.

3   All or a substantial percentage of the day's transactions should be reviewed for accuracy and authenticity and traced to their final disposition.

4   Where applicable, as in the case of loans, letters of credit and so forth, all supporting documentation should be reviewed for authenticity and proper execution.

5   Requests for confirmation of cash balances, items in the process of collection or transfer, outstanding loan balances, and securities held in safekeeping or as collateral for loans should be sent to customers, bank agents, clearing banks, correspondent banks, and so forth. Confirmation requests should not be sent to trust beneficiaries or other interested parties to the trust because the bank as trustee is totally responsible and liable. It should be noted that even if a customer responds with a positive answer to a confirmation request, the bank is not relieved of liability if the customer should later decide, with proof, that the bank had made a mistake.

Comprehensive examinations as of a given date do provide management with some assurance that as of that date, all assets, liabilities, and income due have been accounted for. If the examination has been conducted thoroughly and professionally, there is a good chance of uncovering fraud, errors, losses, or potential liability because only one function or department has been examined, and all the forces of the internal auditing department have been directed at that particular function or department. It is, of course, very time-consuming, and to be effective requires much dedicated follow-up. The fiduciary departments are the exceptions to the efficacy of the examination approach. It is not possible, except for securities held in safekeeping, to conduct an examination of an entire trust department. Most fiduciary liability rests with the bank as executor or trustee; to uncover liability in a bank's administration of an estate or trust requires a detailed analysis of every governing instrument in light of applicable statutory laws and the general law of trusts. This can only be accomplished through a sound administrative review of all fiduciary accounts by the auditing department over a period of time.

ANALYSIS AND EVALUATION OF ACCOUNTING, OPERATING, AND CONTROL SYSTEMS ESTABLISHED TO PROVIDE BANKING SERVICES AND CARRY OUT BANKING FUNCTIONS

It has been shown that the audit of every transaction and account is, in most instances, neither feasible nor desirable. The internal bank auditor therefore is faced with the problem of how to make reasonably certain that each transaction is valid and has every chance of being accurately and safely processed. This is no different from the problem confronting manufacturers of products consumed and used by the public, except for one inescapable reality, which is that the banker uses other peoples' money to produce the services the public wants. The banker is forced to be even more cautious than the manufacturer.

Does the manufacturer test every item that comes off the assembly line? Obviously, this would be impossible, and from a cost point of view, prohibitive. (Durable consumer goods such as cars, trucks, and other life-menacing items are in a separate class and are excluded from this discussion.) For the most part, the astute business man makes certain that: the machinery used in manufacturing is of the best quality; the operating system is efficiently designed to save time and effort; the quality-control tests are adequate and precisely performed; the materials used are of the best quality; the people manning the system are well-trained; and those in key and supervisory positions know the business from the ground up.

The banker must approach the development and production of services and the execution of banking functions in the same way. Knowing that every transaction cannot be monitored and realizing that error, fraud, and embezzlement are always possible, the operations manager must see to it that systems and procedures are efficiently designed and effectively controlled, and that staffing is adequate, well trained, and well supervised. This is the first line of defense. The second line of defense is the auditor, whose responsibility it is to make sure that the first line is all that it should be, or that the operations managers have fulfilled their responsibility.

The auditor has three choices: one, to concentrate solely on the systems of control; two, to concentrate on the operating, accounting, and processing procedures; and three, to bring them all together under one comprehensive and detailed analysis and appraisal. From a practical point of view, the third choice would seem to be the best because it takes as much effort and time to analyze and appraise controls as it does to cover the accounting and operating systems and procedures. To be convinced, all the auditor has to do is consider and answer two questions:

1   Is it possible to accurately analyze and evaluate systems of control without reviewing and analyzing the accounting and operating systems they support?

2   Could an auditor really render a valid and meaningful opinion on the efficiency of a bank's accounting and operating systems without having also reviewed their supporting systems of control?

The answer to both questions is "No"! The two are intertwined and must be reviewed together. Systems of control cannot be evaluated independently of the operating and accounting systems they support, and no operating or accounting system can be said to be efficient unless it is adequately controlled. That is not to say, of course, that once a thorough and comprehensive analysis has been completed, documented, and updated that the auditor cannot look at the controls from time to time to make sure they are still effective and are being followed. Neither does it mean that under the same circumstances the auditor cannot look at the operating and accounting systems to make sure there have been no unauthorized changes or laxity in compliance. Authorized changes can also be evaluated with respect to their effect upon existing controls. However, when a review, analysis, and appraisal are being done for the first time, or for the first time in several years, the accounting and operating systems and their procedures and controls should be reviewed simultaneously if a sound appraisal is to be made.

Review Objectives

These reviews have several objectives.

1   To determine the effectiveness of the control systems supporting the accounting and operating systems for each function and service.

2   To determine the efficiency and quality of the operating and accounting systems designed to carry out each function and produce each service for the purpose of improving these systems, thereby improving service and increasing profitability.

3   To evaluate the performance of the supervisory and operating personnel and their degree of compliance with official policies and applicable laws.

Review Procedure

1   Interviews must be planned and scheduled with the official, supervisory, and clerical staff to obtain detailed data on the organization of the department or division, including the respective responsibilities of each level and its members, as well as a thorough description of each step in the accounting, operating, and control systems involved in the function and/or service.

2   The auditor then must prepare complete narrative descriptions of the systems from the data collected and put them in formal written form. They should then be referred to the official, supervisory, and clerical staff for review, correction, and final mutual agreement. This step is absolutely necessary to avoid misunderstandings and to produce constructive results. If everyone makes a contribution to the effort and the auditor succeeds in creating an atmosphere of cooperation rather than fear, the whole experience can be rewarding.

3   All of the accounting, operating, and control systems should then be flowcharted to present a graphic illustration of the systems so that they may be more easily analyzed, reviewed, and mutual agreement reached on the accuracy of the presentations.

4   The systems should be analyzed for weaknesses, such as lack of logic in the processing steps or duplication or

unnecessary steps, and an opinion reached as to the systems' adequacy, efficiency, and effectiveness.

5   The daily operations should be observed and departures from approved procedures noted, as well as any difficulties experienced in the course of the processing.

6   The actual transactions just processed should be sampled to determine their validity, the accuracy of their disposition, and whether they support the auditor's findings on the analysis of the systems. Strong points should be noted as well as weaknesses.

7   Recommendations for correction of weaknesses and improvement of the systems should be developed.

8   A formal written report of the entire review procedure, including the auditor's recommendations, should be prepared and directed to the officer in charge of the function or service, with a copy to the directors' examining and audit committee.

This is one of the most effective ways the auditor has of making as certain as possible that every transaction has the very best chance of being processed correctly and that the systems are efficient, effectively controlled, and comply with official bank policy and applicable laws and regulations. It is also a graphic and positive method of convincing management and the operating staff of the need for change if it is necessary. Moreover, it increases the auditor's knowledge, sharpens the auditor's perception and analytical ability, and is one way that the auditor can make a measurable contribution to the profitability of a bank.

There are some disadvantages to this approach, however. Only an auditor with wide experience, a detailed knowledge of banking functions and systems design, and superior analytical abilities can conduct an audit of this kind. The auditor must also be very familiar with bank policies and applicable banking laws and regulations. The auditor must be very tactful and command respect to avoid conflict with operations and management.

This systems approach is very time-consuming. However, if it is properly documented and its data maintained on a current basis, it can serve as a foundation for more frequent and far simpler sampling audits in subsequent periods. The periodic use of questionnaires based on the data collected and the findings will help to keep the data current if they are signed by accounting and operating management. Analytical reviews such as this might not need to be done more than once every two years, depending on the number of systems changes and changes in the management of the operating and accounting areas. This of course can vary, depending on circumstances and the errors and departures from prescribed procedures uncovered by the auditor on periodic tests.

Spot Audits

These are periodically scheduled tests of transactions, accounts, controls, and systems in every banking function and service. They are employed for protection, to keep in touch with current performance, to uncover developing trouble spots, and to prevent and detect errors and fraud.

Statistical Sampling

This is a science that can be extremely useful to auditors. It cannot, however, be treated adequately within the scope of this text, nor is it the purpose of this text to do so. There are many very informative and useful texts on the subject, and the professional auditor would do well to become intimately acquainted with them. It is necessary nevertheless to introduce the subject to those readers who might not have thought of it as a valuable auditing tool.

When an auditor wants to select what is generally referred to as an adequate sample of transactions or accounts, it could be rather difficult to determine what constitutes an adequate sample. First of all, the sample ought to be representative of the entire body of transactions or accounts under audit, that is, it ought to reflect most of the peculiarities or attributes of that population that are significant. For example, if the population consists of commercial deposit accounts, some of the characteristics the auditor should be concerned with are size and volume of transactions, services performed, type of customer (commercial or savings bank, nonbanking corporation, public agency, charitable organization, university, or church), the manner in which the customer pays for its services (compensating balances or fees) and the geographic area represented, which would indicate the account officer involved.

All of these factors have a bearing on the error patterns the auditor would want the sample to disclose. The number of transactions or accounts to be selected would have a bearing on the percentage of errors that would be acceptable. It should be pointed out that in high-volume banking services, even one-half of one percent could be considered unacceptable. As a matter of fact, such a low error rate in some services could even be damaging to a bank's customer base. Sampling in the banking industry is often a very controversial matter. However, since it has been established that all transactions cannot and should not be audited, sampling is the only reasonable alternative if it is coupled with intensive systems analysis.

Having reviewed several possible approaches for the internal bank auditor to use, the question is which one is the most effective. There ought not to be any doubt that a judicious combination of periodic comprehensive examinations, thorough systems analysis, and periodic spot audits and tests using confirmation requests and statistical sampling in all three approaches is the best alternative. However, internal bank auditing, no matter how skillfully it is planned and carried out, and no matter how competent and well-informed the auditors are, is no guarantee that error, fraud, and embezzlement will be uncovered or prevented. There is no such thing as a twenty-four hour vigil by the auditing department; even if there were, it probably would not uncover error and fraud. Most fraud and error are stumbled upon, but the mere fact that there is a competent auditing staff carrying out a comprehensive and intensive auditing program motivates employees to be more alert and careful and acts as a psychological deterrent to would-be perpetrators of fraud, theft, and embezzlement. It has one other very important advantage. Should loss occur in spite of the auditor's best efforts, a bank's insurance carriers and state and federal regulatory authorities cannot accuse the bank of negligence; thus its insurance coverage is secure.

Earlier in this chapter mention was made of a current, much-discussed embezzlement in the Wells Fargo Bank. In this case, an operations officer embezzled about $21,300,000 over a two-year period, purportedly without any help from anyone in the bank. This remains to be proved. There are really not very many definitive details forthcoming from Wells Fargo, and probably there ought not to be. But what is known indicates that serious violations of very basic internal controls existed and that a very poor job was done in designing the bank's interbranch settlement system and procedures. A summary of some of the facts that stand out follows.

1   Wells Fargo had a so-called computerized interbranch settlement account system that was supposed to reconcile interoffice debits and credits. The bank has almost four hundred branches and the volume is crushing. The computer system was designed and programmed to allow five business days to elapse before off-setting debits and credits were reconciled. There was also a limit of

$1,000,000 on the amount of individual entries. When an entry of this amount was processed, the computer "sounded an alarm." The embezzler was keenly aware of both these facts, either because he had worked in the computer area at one time or because there was a leak in security in the computer department.

2 The embezzler entered debits into the settlement account for credit to about thirteen accounts set up for one customer. The off-setting credits were not processed until just before the five days had elapsed and then new debits were immediately entered to back up the credits. The amounts were always under $1,000,000. This is a form of kiting, and a unique one. It was also a very dangerous one for the embezzler because he always had to be on the scene to keep the debits and credits flowing at just the right time.

3 The embezzler was not known to have ever taken the mandatory two-week vacation that was intended to disclose just such a situation as this. If he did, he must have had an accomplice to cover him, or else was able to gain entrance into the bank with his own set of keys.

4 He was not a senior officer and yet was able to process these entries without any second signature of approval. There apparently was no dual control or proper managerial supervision.

5 There was no rotation of key employees in the branch system.

6 The embezzler was personally involved with the accounts in question, which is clearly a case of conflict of interest and should not be permitted.

He was finally tripped up by his own mistake when he entered a credit ticket instead of a debit; the pressure was probably getting to him. An operations clerk called him to get an explanation and when it proved unsatisfactory to her, alerted the auditing department. How this could have continued for over two years in the face of branch audits and examinations has not been made clear and probably never will be. It must be stressed that contrary to what the press or public relations people from Wells Fargo have stated, this was not a computer error or weakness. The blame must be placed at the feet of the people who designed the system and those who approved it. Was the auditor part of the systems design? A computer does exactly what it is programmed to do, no more and no less. People design and program computer systems. If this had been a manual system, the result would probably have been the same unless there was a very alert and perceptive person on board. It is not fair to comment upon the auditor's part in this affair because not enough is known.

5

Application of the Internal Audit Examination and the Analysis of Systems and Procedures to the Commercial Lending Function

A conceptual discussion of auditing philosophy, objectives, approaches, and techniques with no demonstration of how they might be applied to a specific banking function tells only part of the story. It is comparable to a rough sketch on canvas without the forms, details, colors, and shadows of the final painting. The imagination takes over and completes the picture, but not in the way that the artist intended. Imagination is definitely a desirable attribute of the professional auditor, but at this point the significant details of an internal auditing examination of a familiar banking function and an analysis and appraisal of the systems and procedures employed in carrying out that function will help the general reader more than imagination will.

Commercial lending is familiar to the general public. There cannot be many people who are not aware that banks, other corporations, wealthy individuals, and business enterprises of all kinds borrow money for business reasons. Some readers closer to banking also know that commercial loans have always been and continue to be a major source of earnings for commercial banks.

Commercial loans are very different from installment or personal loans, both with respect to the basis on which credit is granted and in the terms of the lending agreement.* Loans are short term, demand, or term, the latter often being secured by collateral because of the risk involved. Frequently loans are guaranteed by third parties. There are also revolving credits and combination term loan/revolving credit arrangements. Lines of credit are also extended to customers who then may or may not borrow on these lines as they see fit. The money is simply being made available at a price and may be used as long as the customer's credit status remains substantially the same. The purchase of a corporation's commercial paper or the purchase of securities under an agreement to resell to the seller at a fixed

*See Chapter 3.

price and at a future time are also regarded by banking
regulatory authorities as commercial loans.

INTERNAL AUDITING EXAMINATIONS OF THE COMMERCIAL LENDING FUNCTION

An examination of a banking department, division, function,
or service is exactly what the word "examination implies. It
is a comprehensive and intensive review and appraisal of all
accounting and operating records, files, documents, items of
value, and proofs and controls, including substantial tests of
transactions and accounts as of a given date. In addition,
requests for confirmation of balances or loans outstanding
and supporting collateral are mailed to customers to make
certain that everything is in order as of the date of the
examination.

Scope of the Examination

The examination covers two distinct phases of the lending
function:

1 The review and appraisal of the adequacy and quality of
   the accounting and operating systems and procedures
   and their underlying controls as disclosed by the accuracy of the loan records and control accounts, both
   the departmental and the general ledger controls accounts, as well as the timeliness of the processing and
   the recording.
2 The review and appraisal of the administration of the
   lending function as revealed by the adherence of lending
   officers to the policies, procedures, controls, and legal
   requirements governing the extension of credit to new
   and existing customers.

Objectives of the Examination

The objectives of the internal audit examination are to determine the following:

1 That the official bookkeeping records in the loan operations division reflect a dollar amount of loans outstanding that is in agreement with the asset account on the general ledger, and that the amount also truly represents all the money the bank has loaned out to bona fide customers.

2 That all required documentation for each loan is on file and in order.

3 That collateral for secured loans is adequate in amount, meets the bank's standards of quality, and is in negotiable form; that is, stock and bond powers have been signed in blank, one for each stock and bond certificate.

4 That the collateral is safely housed and strictly controlled.

5 That payments of principal, interest, and fees are being received on time and in accordance with the provisions of the governing loan agreements, and that they are being credited promptly to the appropriate general ledger accounts.

6 That bank lending policies and procedures are being followed.

7 That legal requirements are being met.

8 That the loans outstanding and lines of credit constitute prudent and profitable investments of depositors' funds.

9 That loans in arrears as to principal, interest, or fees are being followed; action is being taken where circumstances so indicate; and adequate reserves against actual and possible losses are being maintained.

10 That where compensating balances are required instead of fees, the balances being maintained are adequate.

Examination of Loan Operations

Preparation

If the examination is to have a fighting chance in detecting fraud, embezzlement, error, departures from approved operating policies and procedures, and violations of statutory and regulatory requirements, it must not be scheduled as of the end of the month or calendar quarter. Perpetrators of fraud, theft, and embezzlement are more likely to try to cover their tracks at these times in anticipation of the auditors' arrival. It is imperative therefore that all audits and examinations be conducted on a "surprise basis" so that the perpetrators can be taken unawares as much as possible, making it easier to disclose actual or potential loss. Admittedly, this is a very difficult standard to maintain because operating personnel, officers, and directors are always on the alert for the appearance of internal and outside auditors, and the dishonest have an uncanny instinct for diverting the auditors' attention. Every effort therefore must be made to preserve that strategic element of surprise.

The auditor may want to prepare a list of questions for operating management and personnel to answer, but it is preferable for the auditors to dig out the answers on their own by observation, testing, and questioning. The preparation of such a list of questions is nevertheless recommended as a guide for the auditors. The list should cover accounting and operating procedures and controls, bank policy, and legal requirements. It should be prepared well in advance of the examination and discussed in detail with the entire auditing staff.

The procedures, findings, and recommendations disclosed in the workpapers of the previous examination and in the reports on the examinations conducted by the state and Federal Reserve Bank Examiners (National Bank Examiners for national banks) should be reviewed and studied carefully. The weaknesses noted in both examinations and the corrective measures recommended should be given special attention. During the examination, tests should be made in the specified areas of weakness and systems should be studied to determine whether corrective action was taken as recommended. If the weaknesses previously cited are still evident and if little or no corrective action was taken, it should be stressed in the final report on the current examination.

The examination should be conducted and supervised by senior, experienced auditors. Newly hired or junior auditors must of necessity assist under senior guidance as they learn through observation on the job and through formal training given by the auditing department to new recruits. The entire auditing staff assigned to the examination should be briefed well in advance on the procedures and techniques to be employed, the reasons for their selection, the objectives of the examination, and of course on the subject matter of the function to be examined.

Procedure

1   At the beginning of the examination, the auditors must establish physical control over all the records, collateral, entries being processed, and all supporting documentation to prevent any attempt to cover up fraud, embezzlement, theft, violations of bank policy, operating procedures, and statutory and regulatory requirements.

2   If the examination is to take place as of the close of business that day, control should be established by stationing auditors in every strategic operating area so that they may observe the completion of the day's processing; for example, the routing and recording of all debits and credits and all deposits and withdrawals of collateral. When operating personnel have completed all interdepartmental transmittals and other proofs and all trans-

action journals, the auditor should take over and begin verifying these proofs.

If the examination is to take place as of the opening of business the following morning, all records, collateral and proofs should be placed in the vault under the auditor's seal. The next morning, the auditors should be on hand before the opening of business to make sure that the auditor's seal is not broken and that the work of the day begins on time.

When examining a function such as commercial lending, there is no better time to schedule an examination than as of the close of business on a Friday. The examination can then be carried out over the weekend. As a matter of fact, if at all possible, all examinations of this size and scope should be scheduled for weekends because the pressures created by the disruptions of daily business are absent and there is more time to conduct the examination calmly and with greater thoroughness. Operating management and personnel will, of course, have to be present, which never makes the auditor very popular.

3 All departmental subsidiary accounting and operating records such as outstanding loans, commitments, contingent liabilities, accounts receivable, interest and/or fee income and suspense, or funds held awaiting payment, should be run and proved to departmental controls and to the respective general ledger accounts. This preliminary and very necessary procedure gives the auditor reasonable but not conclusive proof that all loans and other customer liabilities are under control and thus subject to audit review, that departmental subsidiary records and the corresponding general ledger accounts are in agreement, and that only valid customer liabilities are reflected thereon.

If the loans are automated, the auditor should have the electronic data processing auditor prepare a computer program that when run against the master loan files will produce a computer printout or trial balance of all customer liabilities on the bank's books. This is infinitely preferable to using the data center program because if someone is engaged in fraud or embezzlement and also has access to the data center or an accomplice in the data center, it is very easy for that person or the accomplice to modify the program to suppress the printout of the fraudulent loans or those loans from which funds have been diverted so as to eliminate them from the examination procedure and thus keep them under cover.

The total amount of customer liabilities shown on the computer printout should be verified with the departmental subsidiary controls and with the general ledger accounts. It should be understood that agreement with subsidiary departmental contols and the general ledger does not mean the auditor may assume that the records actually reflect only bona fide loans made by the bank. Unauthorized, fraudulent, or manipulated loans might very well be included in either manual or automated records and not be readily apparent to the auditor. The auditor's job is to find them, determine what weaknesses in procedures and controls contributed to their existence; or more likely, who failed to comply with approved procedures and controls and how the person or persons managed to do so without being stopped. The final and sometimes most difficult problem to unravel is the method of concealment used and the failure of both internal and outside auditors to uncover the fraud, theft, or embezzlement during previous audits and examinations.

4   The total dollar amount of the day's transactions as evidenced by the journal or departmental copies of the posting transaction tickets should be run and proved to the corresponding dollar amounts passed to the various bookkeeping areas and to the general ledger account in the controller's department. These interdepartmental

transactions should be recorded on formal interdepartmental transmittal or proof sheets and supported in the bookkeeping areas by the original copies of the transaction posting tickets.

5 A substantial sample of the day's transactions should be selected at random, reviewed for accuracy (where possible) and proper authorization, and traced to their final disposition and recording in the proper accounts. These accounts would include customers' loan accounts, customers' deposit accounts, customers' custodian accounts where liens against securities held are either placed or removed, bank income accounts for interest and/or fees, accounts receivable, and suspense accounts, or accounts for funds held awaiting payment.

6 A representative sample of loans should be selected from the manual or automated records for intensive review. The method or selection will vary but should include such criteria as the size of the loan, the industry of the borrower, the purpose of the borrowing, the type of loan, and the lending group or officer. There are other criteria that could be used for selecting loans for review; for example, special attention should be given to loans in default as to payments of principal and/or interest. However, it is not the purpose of this chapter to discuss the various technical aspects of sampling, which is a study by itself, but to give the general reader an idea of how a sampling strategy based on common sense and intimate knowledge of a function might produce a fairly decent composite picture of the commercial lending situation in a particular bank. It should give the auditor an opportunity not only to review specific loans, but also to review a cross-section of the commercial lending department, thus making it possible to analyze and evaluate the general performance and management of that function. The auditor should also have a better chance of uncovering departures from approved lending policy, procedures,

and controls and possibly actual theft, fraud, and embezzlement.

For the loans selected, all document and credit files should be examined carefully to ascertain that the loans were granted in accordance with approved procedures, that the files contain the required documentation, and that the operating records accurately reflect all the necessary information needed to ensure smooth processing and follow-up throughout the term of the loan.

Each loan operating record should show the following:

a   The name and address of the borrower.

b   The date the loan was made and the original amount of the loan.

c   The type of loan, that is, term, short term, or demand, and secured or unsecured.

d   Maturity, where applicable.

e   The name of the guarantor if the loan is guaranteed.

f   The rate of interest payable and the frequency of payment.

g   Periodic payments on the loan principal, where applicable.

h   Fees payable or compensating balances due in lieu of fees.

Each document file should contain the following items:

a   A promissory note signed by the borrower with the borrower's signature guaranteed by the lending officer.

b   A properly signed loan agreement with the borrower's signature approved by the lending officer.

c   Where applicable, the board of directors' corporate resolution authorizing the loan and designating the officers authorized to execute agreements on behalf of the corporation.

d The legal review and approval of the loan agreement, including counsel's statement indicating compliance with applicable statutory laws and regulations.

e Credit reviews of the borrower's financial condition at the time of the original borrowing or extension of a line of credit and at the time of all subsequent borrowings.

f A statement explaining the purpose of the loan and the source of funds for repayment.

g Approval of collateral if the loan is secured.

h Approval of the guarantor if the loan is guaranteed, the guarantee signed by the guarantor, and the guarantor's signature approved by the lending officer.

i Audited, periodic financial statements of the borrower if required by the terms of the loan agreement and in keeping with prudent loan surveillance.

j Periodic credit reviews made to keep abreast of the borrower's financial condition.

7 All securities held as collateral for secured loans should be counted, proved to the customers' records and departmental controls, and examined for authenticity and negotiability in case the borrower defaults on the loan and the bank has to sell the securities to recover its money. Stock and bond powers signed in blank for each certificate held should be on file, but not together with the actual securities. This would make it much too easy for a dishonest employee to liquidate the securities for his or her own benefit. All substitutions of collateral should be approved by the security analysts and the lending officer before they are accepted.

If the securities pledged belong to a third party, that is, if someone other than the borrower agreed to pledge them, the auditor should make certain that they have been signed over to the bank under hypothecation agreements. If the securities pledged are held in the borrower's or third party's custodian bank account, the auditor should verify their physical existence in either of those accounts and make certain they have been liened on the securities ledgers and segregated to prevent inadvertent withdrawal. If the securities are held by another bank, there should be certifications in the file from that bank acknowledging that they are holding the securities for the lending bank as collateral to the loan.

All securities should be priced using prices published in financial journals or reputable newspapers such as *The New York Times* and the *Wall Street Journal*. In the case of unlisted securities, such as some over-the-counter stocks and bonds, or securities just not traded the day of the examination, such as some municipal bonds, the auditor will have to obtain prices in writing from two or more reputable brokers or dealers. The market value of the collateral as of the date of the examination should comply with the loan/value ratio requirements set by the bank. If it is only equal to or less than the outstanding loan balance, the matter should be referred to the commercial lending management immediately and, of course, included in the final report on the examination.

If life insurance policies are being held as collateral, there should be written evidence in the files from the insurance carrier that premium payments are current or the policies paid up and that they have been assigned to the bank as collateral. The auditor must make certain that the cash surrender value of the policies equals the outstanding loan balances, because if the loan should be seriously in arrears and the bank should have to turn in the policies, it will receive the cash surrender value and not the face value. In cases where the success of a business totally depends on the efforts or unique expertise of one or two individuals, the bank will undoubtedly demand that they provide life and disability insurance in which the bank is designated as the beneficiary.

8 Each loan should be reviewed to be sure that it is current with regard to required payments of principal, interest, fees, or compensating balances as provided for in the loan agreement.

9 Requests for confirmation should be prepared and sent to all borrowers and credit line customers. The requests should cover the amounts outstanding; the lines of credit granted; arrears in payments on loans, interest, and fees; and balance deficiencies in cases where compensating balances are required or collateral has been pledged to secure loans. Confirmation requests should also be sent to third parties who are either guarantors of loans or have pledged collateral to secure them and, of course, to other banks that are holding collateral pledged to secure loans made by the lending bank.

A follow-up must be performed for answers to these requests for confirmation. The requests should be positive, that is, the customer or third party should be asked to respond in writing not only if something is wrong but also if the facts stated are correct. It is advisable to send out a second request if the initial response is too small. It is very doubtful that the requesting auditor will receive a 100-percent return; an 80-percent response would probably be considered satisfactory by most auditors. All confirmation requests should include stamped, self-addressed envelopes and should be taken directly to the post office by two or more members of the auditing staff. Confirmation requests should not be placed in the bank's own mailing system because a request might be intercepted by someone who is involved in fraud or embezzlement or who has taken or diverted funds that should have been applied to a loan or credited to an earnings account.

Requests for confirmation reveal many things such as

incorrect addresses, customers who have moved and left no forwarding addresses (unlikely where corporations are concerned and the account officer keeps in close touch with the customer), incorrect outstanding loan balances, payments of interest or fees that were not recorded, and so forth. They are a powerful tool for uncovering fraud, theft, and embezzlement, provided the request gets into the right hands. This is a problem, particularly when there is collusion between a bank officer or employee and an officer or employee of the customer, or where an employee of the bank is simply negligent. However, if the request for confirmation does reach the right person and does not reflect loan, interest, or fee payments that were really made, or if the cited collateral does not include collateral that the bank should be holding, strong protests are certain to be forthcoming. This does help to reveal honest error, theft, fraud, and embezzlement.

There are some situations in which a confirmation request will not be effective, such as in the case of fraudulent loans made by a lending officer to an accomplice or to himself or herself using an alias. In this case, the perpetrators will respond and will usually satisfy the auditor. Other auditing techniques therefore must be employed to uncover situations of this kind. These techniques are usually reviews of the procedures for granting and recording a loan and careful sampling of loans put on the books since the last audit or examination. In selecting the sample, the auditor must be able to select loans made by all lending officers.

During the course of an examination, the auditor must be constantly on the alert for departures from approved procedures and controls, such as permitting an employee who bills customers to also process checks and cash and to record such entries on the bank's books. Another example of the absence of strategic control is to allow those who physically receive and withdraw collateral at customers' requests to also record these transactions on the customers' ledgers. The basic principle of control involved in the foregoing situations is a most fundamental and critical control known as "segregation of duties" which prevents any single individual from completing a transaction from its inception to its completion. It is not, however, a safeguard against internal collusion, and should be supplemented by rotation of employees, mandatory two-week vacations away from the bank, and strict supervision and enforcement of these controls. The failure to set up such controls and to enforce them throughout an operating system is to open the door to theft, fraud, embezzlement, and error. However, they are not guarantees, but only deterrents that make it more difficult for the dishonest and the negligent. They also prove that the bank is acting prudently and is not guilty of negligence in managing its operations.

There are other internal operating and accounting controls needed for safe, efficient, and error-free loan operations and accounting systems. The experienced auditor is familiar with these controls and is aware of what must be kept in mind throughout an examination. The controls have been discussed in Chapter 3, The Nature of the Control Function, but it is important to stress what has been said before, that the controls required by a specific system and organization cannot be detailed in advance as a rigid format. Everything depends on the design of the system, the organizational structure of the bank and the commercial loan department, and the policies and guidelines established by management.

Examination of Management and Administration

The examination of management and administration has very special basic objectives. It is quite apparent from an analysis and evaluation of these objectives that the examination cannot be carried out as of a given point in time, that is, as of the date of the examination. It is also obvious that the internal auditing department requires a staff of credit specialists to handle the very technical requirements of this type of examination. The objectives are several:

1 To determine whether there are any deteriorating loans in the bank's portfolio of which management is not aware.

2 To make certain that adequate loan-loss reserves have been established to cover not only realized losses but those loans where there is a high probability of loss in the immediate future.

3 To determine whether the percentage of such actual and probable losses endangers the financial stability of the bank.

4 To make certain that management either has taken or is in the process of taking definitive action as required.

5 To determine that there has been compliance with applicable statutory laws and regulations.

Management's overriding objective is the attainment of a loan portfolio that is safe, optimally profitable in light of money market rates, and a prime investment for its depositors and stockholders. This objective cannot be achieved unless management has formulated and put into writing sound lending policies covering, among other things, types of loans preferred, defined geographic marketing areas, acceptable collateral and the ratio of its market value to the amount of the loan, the pricing of loans, and loan portfolio diversification, servicing, accounting procedures, and procedures for handling delinquent loans.

Guidelines must also be set for credit analysis and evaluation of the financial condition of a potential or current borrower on the basis of which extensions of credit can be granted or refused. These same guidelines and standards should be applied in the continuing review and appraisal of borrowers and the terms of their loan agreements from the first day of the loan to the loan's expiration. Management must also set lending limits for each level of lending officer and requirements for loan approval by their superiors. There is no question but that the caliber of a bank's lending officers and credit analysts plays an important part in management's policy decisions on lending. It is probably as important as adequacy of capital and deposits. Intelligence, knowledge, and expertise as well as a talent for recognizing or "smelling out" troubled waters before they actually appear are invaluable qualifications for a lending officer or credit analyst.

There are differing opinions on the question of who should be responsible for the essential continuing review and evaluation of the borrower's financial condition and the provisions of the loan agreement in light of changing economic conditions. The banking industry has learned the hard way that loans do not just die out overnight and that a continuing review is indispensable in maintaining a healthy loan portfolio. There is always advance warning of trouble, if someone is only on the alert to catch the signals. There is no sitting back and relying on past analyses if disaster is to be avoided.

The internal auditor's independence from interference by operating management and the sale's arm of the bank, and his or her noninvolvement in the performance of the lending function would appear to make the internal auditor the most desirable candidate for the job. Actually, there is no real reason the auditing department cannot carry out this critical function, providing management is willing to underwrite the establishment of a specialized technical group devoted to just this task. The internal auditor reports to the Directors' Examining and Audit Committee and not to lending management; therefore, it is much more likely that a truly objective analysis and appraisal of the borrower's financial condition and the terms of the loan agreement would be made. However, there might be some problems if the internal auditor is unaware of some of the subtle but significant lending considerations because he or she has never been involved in actual lending. The same criticism, however, could be applied to any specialized group set up to do the job, including the credit analysts. Nothing in banking that makes it successful is totally learned from textbooks or technical manuals. It is achieved through years of experience and sometimes through bitter trial and error.

Some banks have established credit audit departments that also report to the Directors' Examining and Audit Committee and are composed of credit specialists who work with the internal auditor. Management probably feels that because of the critical nature of the commercial lending function, it deserves a specialized group of auditors. The credit auditors review and evaluate the original credit analysis made by the lending credit analysts. They also carry out the ongoing review and analysis of the borrower's financial condition and the provisions of the loan agreement in light of any significant changes in the economic and money market scenes. There are some bankers who believe that the lending officer should review the loans because he or she is closer to the borrower, knows the borrower's financial problems better than anyone else, and can therefore detect changes more readily. This is probably true, but having made the loan, the lending officer might not be able to be objective or even willing to invite criticism from management for what might turn out to have been a bad decision. Even if a lending officer reviews the loans made by another lending officer, the review is inevitably made from the point of view of one whose job it is to make loans and take risks. This conditioning is not particularly conducive to producing an objective opinion. The fact remains, however, that no matter who is assigned to do the job, the internal auditor still has the responsibility of making certain that it is done and that management is informed of the results.

ANALYSIS AND EVALUATION OF COMMERCIAL LENDING SYSTEMS

It has been established that the safety and efficiency of the systems designed to carry out the processing and accounting procedures that support the functions and services of a bank are the first priorities of management and the primary concern of the internal auditor. It is recognized that it is neither possible nor desirable for the internal auditor to audit every transaction or every account. The efficiency and safety of the systems and procedures are the responsibility of operating management; it is the auditor's responsibility to see that operating management is fulfilling this responsibility. The internal auditor does this by reviewing and evaluating the operating and accounting systems to determine whether they are efficient, safe, and give each transaction every opportunity of being properly processed.

Objectives of the Systems Analysis and Evaluation

The objective of systems analysis and evaluation in commercial lending is to improve the efficiency of the systems and procedures supporting commercial loans. This is accomplished by determining several things:

1　Whether the administrative, accounting, and operating systems are accurately and efficiently processing, recording, and servicing new, existing, and terminating loans on the bank's books.
2　Whether these systems can comfortably accommodate a substantial increase in the volume of new business.
3　If these systems and procedures are operating safely because the underlying systems of control are effective.
4　Whether measurable and significant improvements can be made.

Scope of the Systems Analysis

The auditor's review and analysis should cover the following:

1 Administrative policies and procedures governing the extension of credit.
2 Operating and accounting systems and procedures for processing new loans, renewals of existing loans and terminating loans.
3 Accounting systems and procedures for recording other daily transactions such as the accrual and collection of interest, the billing and collection of fee income, payments on loans, and the deposit and withdrawal of securities pledged as collateral.
4 The various systems of control intended to prevent and detect loss.
5 The ability to retrieve information from the records with ease.

Preparation for Conducting the Systems Analysis and Evaluation

Careful planning and preparation coupled with inquisitiveness, imagination, and tenacity will ensure the success of a study of this kind and magnitude. Since the undertaking essentially involves gathering, classifying, and analyzing information, it needs the understanding and support of the management and line personnel of the commercial loan department. It is not possible, therefore, to conduct this study on a surprise basis. It is not an audit in the usual sense of the word; rather, it is a detailed preparation of a firm foundation for subsequent "surprise" audits and examinations. To do a creditable job, the auditor must prepare management and line personnel in advance and enlist their support. It is very time-consuming both for the staff and the auditor and it does interfere with daily operations. Patience, politeness, and persuasion are the auditor's weapons or, perhaps more accurately stated, his "Alladin's lamp."

In preparing for the study, the auditor should gather together all available written material on the commercial lending function covering bank policy, credit analysis, lending procedures, and all administrative and operating procedures. Hopefully, the auditor has already reviewed these materials, such as they may be, during previous audits and examinations. If not, they should now be reviewed and analyzed for completeness, clarity, and compliance with the necessary controls in each phase of the lending function. The auditor should prepare a written record of all weaknesses in these instructions for eventual comparison with the auditor's findings on their adequacy and the degree of compliance by lending officers and line personnel with the prescribed procedures.

The auditing staff selected to carry out this review should for the most part be senior seasoned auditors who are intimately acquainted with the subject matter to be reviewed. They should, of course, be accompanied by junior or uninitiated auditors who will participate under their guidance as part of on-the-job training.

Procedure for Conducting the Systems Analysis and Evaluation

For the purpose of illustration, it is being assumed that an entire review of this nature has not been done before. In practice, this type of review would not be done on an annual basis because to do so, except under extraordinary circumstances, would destroy its purpose and negate its benefits.

1 In performing the study, the auditor in charge should first make an appointment with the executive heading the commercial lending function and the executive in charge of commercial loan operations to acquaint them with the objectives of the review, enlist their support, and obtain a detailed description of their respective organizational structures and the responsibilities of the officers at each subordinate level of management.

2 Organization charts and a narrative description of the organization should then be prepared and referred back to the executives for approval or correction. It would be advisable to have them initial the final products.

3 Using the organization charts as a guide, the auditor should then proceed to interview the officers and supervisors at each subordinate level of management to find out how each level is organized and what the responsibilities are of the people reporting to them. Here again, organization charts as well as narrative descriptions of the segmented functions and their organizational structures should be prepared and referred back to the officers interviewed for their approval and signatures.

4 All line personnel should be interviewed to obtain a detailed description of their duties and the procedures they follow. All of this information should be reduced to a logical, detailed description of each portion of the overall system, highlighting control points or lack thereof, with flow charts graphically portraying the systems and procedures.

5 The narrative descriptions and flow charts should be prepared in multiple copies and distributed to the managing officers, supervisors, and line personnel for review, correction, and final mutual agreement.

6 The auditors should sit down together and analyze the systems, procedures, and flowcharts for weakness in controls and weaknesses in design or work flow. They

should also analyze the capacity, adequacy, and effectiveness of the operating and accounting forms and records.

7   An adequate and representative sample of transactions and accounts should be then selected to be audited for accuracy, authenticity, and compliance with established procedures and controls. Special attention should be paid to the areas of weakness disclosed by the review and analysis of the systems and controls. If the auditors were correct in their analysis and evaluation and if they were lucky in their sampling, the findings uncovered in their testing might support their analysis. If not, they might select another sample; however, the absence of error or indications of fraud or embezzlement in the selected samples does not necessarily mean that their analysis of the system was incorrect. The opportunity for theft, fraud, and embezzlement is enough. The fact that it has not happened probably means that either the bank's staff is honest or the bank has just been lucky for the time being. It could also mean that evidence is buried in other transactions and other accounts.

8   Recommendations for correcting weaknesses in controls and for improving operating and accounting systems and administrative procedures should be prepared and incorporated in the final report to the executives in charge of commercial lending and commercial loan operations. Before the auditor releases the report to these executives and to the Directors' Examining and Audit Committee, a meeting should be held with the executives involved to discuss the contents of the report and to critique the findings and operations.

Areas of Concern to Auditing and Management

Auditing and management share a number of concerns.

1   Policies and procedures governing the extension of credit.

  a   What criteria have been established for extending credit? Are they in writing?

  b   Who has been designated to review the credit analyses and the borrower's application?

  c   What documentation is required for loans that have been approved?

  d   Who has been designated to approve loans along with the lending officer at the various levels of lending authority?

  e   Is there a loan committee before whom all loans must be presented before they are actually paid out?

2   Procedures and controls governing the recording of new loans or the refinancing of existing loans.

  a   Do lending officers use formally prepared forms to advise the commercial loan operations of new loans made and existing loans that have been refinanced?

  b   Has someone other than the lending officer been designated to issue checks upon proper authorization or to credit the customer's deposit account?

  c   Are securities or life insurance policies pledged as collateral recorded on the borrower's records by someone other than the person who physically received them for safekeeping?

  d   Is collateral held under joint custody so that the deposit and withdrawal of collateral cannot be accomplished by a single individual?

  e   Are interest, fees, and payments on loans billed, received, and processed by different individuals?

  f   Are departmental subsidiary records run and proved to the general ledger controls each day by someone other than the person or persons who post them?

  g   Are loans in arrears as to principal payments, interest, and fees being followed by someone other than the person who receives and processes the payments?

3 Work Flow and Processing

    a Are the processing steps in commercial loan operations logically and efficiently designed so that transactions are received and processed without unwarranted duplication of effort?

    b Are the processing steps arranged so that each successive step acts as a check on the preceding step as much as possible?

    c Are daily transaction journals maintained and proven to the interdepartmental transmittal proof sheets at the end of the day?

4 Records and Files

    a Are individual loan records complete as to critical information?

    b Are there permanent files for each loan containing the original authorization to set up the loan record?

    c Do the files contain records of original collateral pledged, copies of approval of collateral, and copies of all subsequent approvals for withdrawal and substitution?

CONCLUSIONS

The areas of concern discussed are not all inclusive because the scope and degree of intensive investigation ultimately depend on the individual policies and systems of each bank. The results of the review and analysis will of course be summarized in a formal report to the executive officers in charge, with a copy to the Directors' Examining and Audit Committee. The report should contain the auditor's opinions and recommendations for corrective action.

The workpapers in the auditor's hands at the conclusion of the systems review and analysis should be made part of a permanent file to be used for subsequent periodic audits of special areas of the commercial lending function and for complete examinations. These workpapers, particularly with regard to the detailed description of the systems, procedures, and controls, should be kept current by subsequent spot reviews and by asking the management of the function to review and either approve the description and flowcharts or to indicate any changes that were made without prior advice to the auditor. All areas in which changes were made should in due course be reviewed and tested by the auditor. This procedure is an invaluable tool for effective auditing and should be carried out in every major area of the bank.

6

Planning the Auditing Program

**Standards
and Guidelines**

Planning a comprehensive auditing program for any bank is not an easy task. The internal auditor as a managerial control must be able to reconcile the auditing program's objectives and evaluation of the degree of protection required in each area of the bank's operations with the management's objectives without destroying the integrity of the auditing function. Even under the best of circumstances, this is a formidable and frustrating undertaking.

Planning is generally a never-ending task no matter what the industry or field of endeavor. It is a continuing activity that must forge ahead to meet the needs of change. Change is probably the only condition on which the auditor may rely. Auditing objectives, approaches, techniques, and schedules must keep pace with both internal and external changing conditions if auditing is to provide the protection that management expects and needs.

The internal bank auditor must cope successfully with many factors, some of which are variables by nature and some of which are affected by external conditions or unexpected events. The internal auditor must keep a sensitive finger on the pulse of the bank and the industry and when planning an overall program must take into consideration a host of variables:

1   Turnover of the auditing staff.
2   Availability of competent auditing personnel.
3   Intelligence, education, and aptitude of auditing personnel.
4   Turnover of operating management and personnel.
5   Competence of operating management and personnel.
6   Changes in the organizational or reporting structure of the various banking functions and departments.
7   The special nature and inherent liability of each banking and trust function.
8   New technological services and systems.

9   The impact of change on the bank's exposure to error and fraud.

10 Budgetary limitations placed on the auditing function by management.

11 Requirements of state and federal regulatory authorities.

12 Requirements of the certified public accountants hired by the board of directors to certify the bank's annual reports.

Planning the structure and details of a function that will focus on and critique the work of other people is a very sensitive and difficult task. The internal bank auditor needs the total support of management and must be independent of all interference from operating management. Ideally, the auditor should report to the chairman of the board of directors either directly or through a Directors' Examining and Audit Committee. The auditor's independence should be assured by supporting provisions in the by-laws of the bank.

The internal auditor also needs the inner assurance and confidence that comes from a thorough understanding of the bank's functions and services and their supporting accounting, operating, and control systems. In addition, the internal auditor must understand the special nature and many facets of the different liabilities incurred by the bank in performing the great variety of services for its customers. No matter what is said about statutes of limitations with regard to agency functions as opposed to fiduciary functions, the fact remains that banking is a quasi-public service industry with all of its implied fiduciary responsibilities and liabilities. In courts of jurisdiction, chances are that the public as the complaining party will be favored over the bank if the impairment of public confidence in banking is at issue. It will not matter that the defending bank was not guilty of negligence or fraud if the surrounding circumstances create the impression that it was. Perhaps this is as it should be, because banks do use customers' money to earn money and it is in the best interest of the industry that they make every effort to keep their skirts clean. They are definitely not comparable to other nonbanking corporations or institutions.

The internal auditor must always be aware of this and be able to communicate it to management because, under certain circumstances, severe budgetary limitations might create the impression that management has been guilty of negligence. On the other hand, knowledgable auditors, bankers, and other business people know full well there is no guarantee that even efficiently designed and effectively controlled systems cannot be circumvented by informed and determined adversaries. Nothing is foolproof. Nevertheless, the existence of an adequate and effective auditing program carried out faithfully by competent auditors can absolve management from an accusation of negligence in the event of loss.

The internal auditor should chart the many sources of risk in the bank so that they will be accorded the proper priority in planning the bank's auditing program. All banking functions are susceptible to loss caused by negligence, incompetence, fraud, and embezzlement; some areas are more likely to suffer loss caused by theft, burglary, armed robbery, and forgery. Ideally, the internal bank auditor is expected to review, analyze, and evaluate everything that goes on. Realistically, this is not possible, at least not within a desirable time frame and considering the inevitable budgetary and staffing constraints. Thus the auditor must set priorities with regard to the audit coverage of all of the bank's operations. The logical approach would be to do the following:

1 Determine the relative degree of risk inherent in each functional area and list them accordingly.
2 Assign frequencies of general audits, examinations, spot

audits, and systems analyses to each function, service, or operation.

3 Allocate available qualified auditors among the functions, services, and operations.

4 Determine the number of additional auditors required to carry out the plan.

5 Compute the additional cost.

6 Evaluate the benefits and risks of not increasing the staff.

7 Reduce the assigned frequencies of general audits, examinations, spot audits, and systems analyses if the evaluation indicates that it might be justified.

8 If not, prepare to convince management that their objectives and/or budget restrictions must be changed.

9 If they are not convinced, advise them in writing of the risks involved and made certain that they respond, acknowledging their acceptance of those risks in writing.

A list of some of the prime sources of risk follows.

Areas Where Negotiable and Nonnegotiable Items of Value Are Handled

Tellers areas and the general cage
Incoming regular and registered mail
Outgoing regular and registered mail
Messengers and armored couriers
Securities processing operations
Custodian department
Fiduciary departments or divisions
    Personal trusts, estates, guardianships, committeeships
    Employee benefit trusts
    Corporate trusts
Bank vault
Commercial, installment, and brokers loan departments
Letter of credit department
Supply department

Areas Where Funds Are Remitted

Tellers areas
Money transfer
Controllers department—accounts payable
Commercial, installment, and brokers' loan departments
Credit card department
Custodian department
Fiduciary departments or divisions
   Personal trusts, estates, guardianships, committeeships
   Employee benefit trusts
   Corporate trusts

Areas Where Funds Are Received

Tellers areas
Money transfer
Controllers department—Accounts Receivable
Commercial, installment, and brokers' loan departments
Credit card department
Mortgage and real estate department
Safe deposit
Custodian department
Letter of credit department
Fiduciary departments or divisions
   Personal trusts, estates, guardianships, committeeships
   Employee benefit trusts
   Corporate trusts

Areas Where Definitive Action Must Be Taken Based On the Bank's Own Judgment

Commercial, installment, and brokers' lending functions
Money market division—resources management
   Management of the bank's own portfolio
   Buying and selling of Federal Reserve funds,
   commercial paper, bankers' acceptances, securities

under agreements to sell or buy back
Foreign Exchange Trading
Fiduciary departments
Personal trusts, estates
Employee benefit trusts

Areas Where Transactions Are Recorded

Demand deposit accounting
Savings account operations
Custodian operations
Trusts operations
Commercial, installment, and brokers' loan operations
Credit card operations
Money market operations
Controllers department—general ledger and subsidiary
accounts
Electronic data processing center

Auditing manuals should be prepared describing the functions, services, and operations covered; the types of audits and examinations to be applied in each case; the frequency of such audits and examinations; and the planning requirements for each audit or examination.

Each audit and examination should always include among other things a review and evaluation of the control systems underlying each function or operation, a review for compliance with applicable statutory laws and regulations, and a review for compliance with bank policies and procedures.

Auditing programs and schedules should be so designed that there is no possibility of their being regarded as control functions, but rather as appraisals of the controls that are the responsibility of operating management and personnel. Maintaining the element of surprise as much as possible will help in great measure to prevent scheduled audits from being substituted for internal and other controls.

7

Auditing Reports and Other Workpapers

One of the tasks that many auditors dislike and resist doing is preparing and organizing the detailed, written records of their audits, examinations, reviews, and appraisals in an orderly fashion. Adequate and skillful documentation of the work of the auditing department is critically important for several reasons, not the least of which is that it constitutes the necessary evidence that the auditor has been carrying out the planned program of audits and examinations on schedule.

The audit function is one of the most difficult to cost-justify, mainly because its effectiveness is not measurable. The auditor cannot prove, for example, that the apparent absence of fraud and error might be the direct result of the audits and examinations that have been performed. Of course the absence or nonsurfacing of error and fraud might be either an accident of timing or, in the case of fraud, the vigilance of the perpetrator. They could be lying there, dormant, waiting to be uncovered, in which case when they are revealed, the auditor will have a difficult time explaining why they were not uncovered in the course of regular audits and examinations. Management is apt to forget that the best of auditing techniques is no guarantee against fraud and negligence; it is simply a prudent course and a deterrent. Without an auditing program and a competent auditor, management would be declared negligent itself in the event of fraud and embezzlement.

On the other hand, an objective review of comprehensive and well-organized workpapers disclosing what the auditor did and how it was done might indicate the very real possibility that the auditing program was indeed a contributing factor in preventing fraud and error. It is in instances of fraud or apparent gross negligence on the part of operations that adequate and understandable working papers recording the events and progress of audits and examinations are of prime importance to management and the internal auditor. If there has been a noticable improvement in a particular operation because the auditor's recommendations were accepted and acted upon, there definitely should be a clear and complete record of that accomplishment in the auditing workpapers for the particular audit or examination.

Documentation of the auditing program, its execution, its findings, and its effect on the operations and services of the bank are important not only to reassure management and to evaluate the competence and dedication of the internal auditor and the auditing staff; it is also of great interest and concern to state and federal bank examiners, other representatives of banking regulatory authorities, and the bank's certified public accountants. These outside auditors' objectives are different from those of the internal auditor. Outside auditors are primarily concerned with the financial stability of the bank and the quality of its management, but they are acutely aware that effective systems of control play an important part in the bank's financial stability and that fraud could be the means of destroying it under certain circumstances. They obviously cannot audit the entire bank in the relatively short time they spend there, so they want to know what the auditor has been doing, what was found in the audits and examinations, what has been done to correct dangerous situations, and how effective the systems of internal accounting and operating controls are. In effect they audit the auditor, and they accomplish this by an intensive review of the auditing workpapers. Since they must rely on the work of the internal auditor, they must be certain that the audit function is adequate and skillfully executed, and that the internal auditor and auditing staff are knowledgeable, competent, and dedicated.

Complete, well-organized, and intelligible workpapers for each audit, examination, or systems study are also very useful in planning subsequent audits and examinations. The auditor planning the next audit or examination will find it very instructive to review the plans of prior audits and examinations, the objectives, the scope, the findings, the recommendations, and the follow-up to find out if action was taken or not taken on the auditor's recommendations. All of these data provide clues as to what the auditor should focus on to find out whether things are better, the same, or worse. While reviewing this record of prior audits, the auditor's imagination is stimulated; the auditor instinctively critiques what has been done and begins to think about improvements, extending the scope of the pending audit or examination and perhaps doing a pre-examination review before finalizing the audit plans.

The training of junior auditors and novices can be greatly enhanced by studying these work papers as a basis for future discussion before embarking on the new audit. The papers should be studied and discussed in detail as part of their pre-audit briefing.

Auditing work papers are also needed occasionally in the event of litigation against the bank.

TYPES OF AUDITING WORKPAPERS

The documentation of an audit or examination begins with the plan of action, the objectives, the scope, the procedures, the sampling approach, and other techniques to be employed. The plans will also cite the people to be interviewed in terms of the organization of the function. Parts of the plans from the previous audit might also be included if they are relevant. Depending on the type of audit, an examination or a systems review, the workpapers would also include the following:

1   Details of interviews with the officers and staff of the operation or function involved.
2   Narrative descriptions of systems, procedures, and controls.

3 Flow charts of administrative, operating, accounting, and control systems.

4 Analyses of these systems, indicating their weaknesses and so forth.

5 Accounts and transactions selected for review.

6 Findings disclosed by the tests of these transactions and accounts.

7 Recommendations for correction and improvement of the systems.

8 Auditing reports sent to the head of the function, system, or service audited with copies to the Directors' Examining and Audit Committee.

9 Replies to these reports.

10 Corrective action taken in response to auditing comments and recommendations.

11 Opinions on the degree of compliance with bank policy and with applicable statutory laws and regulations.

Auditing work papers will also include such items as proofs with subsidiary departmental controls and the general ledger accounts involved. All proofs, schedules of accounts, and transactions should be dated and signed by the auditors who made the proofs, selected the transactions, and accounts, and verified or reviewed them. If requests for confirmation of balances in deposit accounts, outstanding loan balances, or collateral are sent to customers, third parties, or others, a record of those to whom they were sent should be included and the replies documented.

Auditing workpapers should be classified first by the functions audited, second by type of audit (general audit, examination, periodic spot audit, systems analysis, etc.), and then by date. The following is a suggested but not complete list of major functional classifications:

Assets

Cash and due from banks
Loans
   Commercial
   Real estate loans
   Real estate construction loans
   Brokers' loans
   Installment loans
   Credit cards
Investment account securities
Trading account securities
Federal funds sold and securities purchased under resale
   agreements
Accrued income receivable
Due from customers on acceptances
Bank premises
Other real estate
Other assets
   Prepaid expenses
   Funds held awaiting payment
   Other

Liabilities

Demand deposits
   Commercial accounts including banks
   Public funds
   Individual—checking
   Savings
   Trust funds
Time deposits (certificates of deposit)
Short-term borrowings
   Federal funds purchased and securities sold under re-
     purchase agreements
   Commercial paper
   Other

Acceptance outstanding
Accounts payable and accrued liabilities
Long-term debt, debentures, and capital notes
Preferred stock outstanding
Capital stock outstanding
Capital surplus
Retained earnings

Income and Expense accounts

Income
    Interest and fees on loans
    Interest on investment account securities
    Interest on trading account securities
    Interest on federal funds sold and securities purchased
      under resale agreement
    Trust and custodian income
    Commissions on acceptances and letters of credit
    Credit card commissions
    Trading account profits and commissions
    Other operating income
Expenses
    Interest expense on deposits
    Interest expense on borrowings
    Salaries
    Employee benefit expense
    Occupancy expense
    Furniture and equipment
    Other operating expense

Functions, Services and Items of Value Not Reflected on the General Ledger

Trust securities
    Estates and personal trusts
    Employee benefit trusts
    Investment advisory accounts

Custodian account securities
Processing of securities transactions
Inventories of unissued official checks and letters of credit
E Bonds, travelers checks, passbooks, etc.

Other auditing documents that should be on file and are most helpful are copies of the reports of outside examiners such as state and federal bank examiners and the bank's certified public accounting firm.

All auditing work papers should be kept under lock and key in fire-resistant files and retained for at least seven years. Trust audit documentation is another problem and should be kept much longer because there is no statute of limitations on fiduciary liability.

THE AUDIT REPORT

This is the auditor's unique opportunity to communicate with top management. The auditor is a managerial control who serves management and must learn to think in terms of management's objectives. The chairman and the Directors' Examining and Audit Committee are not interested in minor housekeeping errors. They want to know if the assets of the bank are safe; if the various systems installed to carry out the business of the bank are efficient, reliable, and safe; if not, why not; and what will be done to remedy the situation.

The auditing report should not be too long, but should cover the significant facts in a clear and concise manner. The officer or manager in charge of the function audited should know the contents of the written report in advance of its release. It should be addressed to that officer or manager with a copy to the Directors' Examining and Audit Committee.

The report should contain a description of the function audited, the date of the examination, the objectives of the audit or examination, its scope, and the findings. The auditor should also include an opinion covering the adequacy and efficiency of the operating and accounting systems, the effectiveness of the systems of control, the degree of compliance with applicable banking laws and regulations, and adherence to bank policies, regulations, and procedures.

In closing, the auditor should offer recommendations for improving systems, procedures, and controls and request a reply at the officer's earliest convenience.

Auditing work papers are a revealing documentation of the caliber of bank management, the competency of the internal auditor and auditing staff, and the quality of preventive and discovery protection being given to the bank, its assets, liabilities, nonledger functions, and systems and procedures.

8

Auditing Computer Systems and the Data Processing Function

Not too long ago, the internal bank auditor confronted with the prospect of auditing computer systems and the data processing operation was in a position somewhat like that of St. George facing the Dragon. He could not turn and run away, but had to stay and grapple with an unknown and terrifying monster. Unlike St. George, however, he could not slay the monster. The Dragon remained, ever-threatening and always mysterious. He is still here, but things have changed since the monster first appeared. He is no longer so mysterious, but strangely enough, he is more threatening than before. A lot more is known about him now, and that knowledge has made the auditor more acutely aware of his great potential for evil as well as good.

The overwhelming proliferation of automated systems during the past thirty-odd years and the dramatic advances in computer technology have forced the auditor to come to terms with the Dragon and his family of smaller Dragons, the minicomputers and all their peripheral hardware such as magnetic tape drives, disk drives, terminals, and various other items. With experience and training, the auditor now has a better understanding of the nature of the Dragon's astounding power, at the same time recognizing both the limitations and the dangers of that power.

It is interesting to note that in ancient civilizations the Dragon was a symbol of wisdom and fertility; in a way, the twentieth-century Dragon, the computer, resembles the one of days gone by. Although the computer is not exactly re-garded as a repository of wisdom, it has proved to be an awesomely powerful aid in uncovering previously unknown facts and in substantiating or disproving scientific theories. The computer has made it possible to perform complicated calculations in a mere fraction of the many years it would have taken hundreds of scientists and mathemeticians to complete them. Thus the computer, teamed up with man's unlimited imaginative and intellectual capabilities, has made tremendous contributions to the world's store of knowledge in all of man's endeavors.

Without the powerful arm of the computer, man could not have flown into space or walked on the moon in this century. It must not be forgotten, however, that the mind of man conceived the computer, designed and built the computer, and must continue to instruct it on how to operate on the data fed into it. Man still controls the computer, uses it for his own benefit, and hopefully will continue to do so.

Banks have become major users of automation, and the internal bank auditor has many concerns in determining how to approach the audit of computer systems and the data processing operation. Auditing computer systems and auditing the data center and its data processing operations are two entirely different problems. Computer systems are designed and developed by a project team consisting of a project manager, systems analysts, user representatives, programmers, and auditing representatives. The data center takes that system, which is in essence a series of programs or instructions to the computer, and loads it into the computer to perform the accounting and operating functions of the bank. They are two different worlds, and the internal bank auditor must employ auditing techniques suited to each one, or the auditing function will fail to give the bank the protection it needs and expects.

The reasons for auditing computer systems and data processing operations are no different than the reasons for auditing other banking systems and functions. The primary purpose of the auditor is and always will be the prevention and detection of loss caused by negligence and fraud. In either a manual or automated environment, the auditor's purpose is achieved in great part by making certain that the systems involved are efficiently designed, effectively controlled, and incorporate the requirements of the users and the customers.

THE NATURE OF DATA PROCESSING

Whenever the words "data processing" are used, computers and automated systems immediately come to mind, but data has been processed since mankind first learned to use written symbols to communicate and record events. The processing of data in the modern world of business and finance, whether the processing is mechanical, manual, or electronic, involves similar steps or procedures.

The initial data or transactions, known as input, have to be sorted, perhaps by account, classified according to type of transaction or other categories, and purified; that is, either inspected by sight or electronically scanned for errors and inconsistencies. The data then must be proven to the dollar or unit control totals provided by the sending areas. The reasons for these procedures should be obvious. The input sections of the bookkeeping or processing areas must make certain that the data are as error-free as possible before they are actually posted or processed, that all transactions recorded on the accompanying transmittal blotters or tapes have actually been received, and that the input data are organized to facilitate the processing operation.

The data or transactions are then posted, recorded, or otherwise operated upon, and the results of such posting or other operating procedures are either proven to pre-established control totals or recorded on interim proof sheets for verification at a later point in the processing stream.

The end result of processing, also known as the output, could consist of new trial balance listings, statements for customers, reports for internal bank use, or the production of input for other bank processing systems. A familiar example of the last is the periodic preparation of the bank's financial statements, which are prepared from the output of all of the bank's processing systems.

The auditor's approach to the problem of auditing computer systems and the data processing operation must focus on the stages just broadly described, with particular attention to the computer operation that runs the automated systems designed to carry out the work of banking functions and services. The input of data, the operations performed on that input and on the master computer files to which it must be applied, and the final output are all part of the design of what is known as a computer or automated system.

Using the commercial lending function as a means of illustrating what is meant by "input", "processing," and "output" might be helpful in presenting a more vivid picture of these stages of a data-processing system, whether it be manual, mechanical, or electronic.

Input Data or Transactions for Commercial Loans

The input data for commercial loans include, among other items, the following:

1 Instructions to set up accounts for newly opened lines of credit or for new loans.
2 Instructions to close out records of loans that have just been fully paid.
3 Credit tickets to record payments received on existing loans.
4 Credit tickets for recording payments received for interest on loans and fee income in the proper income accounts.
5 Debit tickets for payments on loans, interest, and fees that were collected in accordance with standing authorization to charge the customers' deposit accounts.
6 Instructions to set up records for required collateral on

secured loans and to record the collateral deposited with the bank.

7   Instructions to record withdrawal and substitution of collateral.

Processing the Input for Commercial Loans

This stage involves applying the input transactions to existing loan records, establishing new loan account records, updating subsidiary departmental control records such as total loans outstanding and interest and fee income accounts, closing out the records of fully paid loans, and routing all of the financial data to the general ledger in the controller's department.

Producing the Output

The output is, of course, the end result of the processing of the input and would probably consist of the following:

1   Daily new trial balances of total loans outstanding.
2   Updated loan inventory records reflecting all the critical information about the loan customers and the terms of the loan agreements.
3   Updated records of all collateral held for each secured loan, with new market values for the collateral that can be priced.
4   Reports of loans in arrears on payments of principal, interest, or fees.
5   Updated accounting records of interest earned and fee income.

These are the basic accounting and operating stages of any type of data-processing system. They are particularly critical in automated systems and require the most effective controls. Their design is also a strategic element of the total system. It must incorporate all the requirements of the users and the needs of the customers. It must provide capacity for increased volume and be logically designed for efficient and economical processing. In automated systems, the problem is often staggering. Systems analysts and programmers are not necessarily bankers or even knowledgeable about the function they are preparing to automate. More often than not, they neither understand nor appreciate the need for accounting, operating, and other internal controls. As a matter of fact, they often resist the auditor's insistence that controls be incorporated in the design because their inclusion complicates the design and development effort.

THE ROLE OF MANAGEMENT AND THE AUDITOR IN THE AUTOMATION FUNCTION

The auditor is a managerial control and should receive the full support of management in developing an auditing program for its computer systems and data center. One of management's first duties is to become knowledgeable in the problems and risks of automation and to assume an active role in the organization, management, and coordination of the bank's automation effort. The cost of designing, developing, converting to, and implementing computer systems, of leasing or buying computers and peripheral hardware, and of staffing the computer systems department is enormous, usually running into many millions of dollars. Once the systems are built, they are not easily done over, and sometimes have to be scrapped. Management cannot afford to stand aloof and refuse to get involved. Mistakes and omissions in designing automated systems, in establishing or failing to establish controls, could very well result in additional costs and liabilities that management is not prepared to meet.

The internal auditor must employ several approaches to auditing computer systems and the data processing operation to protect the bank against loss and its customers against invasion of privacy. Negligence and fraud flourish in this environment and are much more difficult to guard against or detect than in nonautomated systems. How can the internal bank auditor accomplish the purpose of internal auditing in an automated environment? What does the internal auditor have to know in order to do it? Is it possible to find an auditor who is a knowledgeable banker, an expert in the field of internal bank auditing, and at the same time understands the technology and hazards of automation? Admittedly, such a person is hard to find. What, then, should a competent and alert banking auditor do to accomplish the task? It has been said that intelligence and education enables an individual to recognize what he or she doesn't know, what he or she ought to know, and where and how to get it. An auditor with this ability can overcome the difficulties of auditing computer systems and the data processing operation.

Auditing Computer Systems

Participation in the Design and Development of Computer Systems

To the degree that budgetary limitations make competent auditors available, the auditing department should plan to participate in the design, development, and implementation of all major automated systems. The internal auditor or a competent representative from the auditing department should be a permanent part of the project team. He or she must first be well grounded in the subject matter of the function to be automated, experienced and competent in auditing, and reasonably well acquainted with the component parts of the central processing units, that is, the computer, systems design, and programming. It is also desirable and advantageous that the auditing representative be an expert in the field of automation; this is not necessary, however, as long as there is such a technically equipped person on the staff of the auditing department who will review the flowcharts of the system, its underlying system of controls, and the programming flow charts or block diagrams with the functional auditor.

As a member of the project team, the auditor must ensure the following:

1 That all current and ultimate users of the proposed system are adequately represented so that the requirements of all users and the needs of the customers will be incorporated into the new system.

2 That adequate and effective input, processing, and output controls are built into the system at the very outset to protect the bank and its customers, to ensure trouble-free and accurate processing, and to make it possible to conduct audits and examinations at a reasonable cost.

3 That adequate test transactions are developed and the results of program and systems' testing are satisfactory.

4 That the conversion to and implementation of the new system are carefully planned and tightly controlled. (This is the stage in which the new system is run in parallel with the old system, if there is one using the same live daily work. Each day's processing must be in proof with the pre-established control totals on both systems, and any exceptions and errors in the new system must be analyzed, corrected, and documented.)

5 That the new system is not permitted to "go operational," that is, that the old system may not be dropped until each member of the project team and management is satisfied with the results of the parallel testing.

6 That there is compliance with the provisions of applicable statutory laws and regulations.

7   That the design, development, and implementation of the
    new system are adequately documented.

Systems Documentation

The documentation of the design, development, and implementation of a computer system is really the history of the
initiation of the system, the exploration of its possibilities,
the planning, the discussions, and the decisions of each
member of the project team, including their final concur-
rence on each and every point at issue. It is a most important set of records, and must be assembled in an orderly,
formal, and permanent manner for future needs. Should
modifications of the system be necessary at some future time
and systems analysts and programmers who built the system
are no longer around, these records would be needed by the
new systems analysts and programmers to find out what was
done and why. Even the analysts and programmers who
were involved in building the system would need the records
to refresh their memories. Bank examiners and the bank's
certified public accountants will also want to review the
records to satisfy themselves that the system was properly
designed and incorporates all the necessary controls.

Equally important, the records will be needed by the
internal auditor so that the electronic data processing auditor
can write computer programs to review the systems, test the
controls and the processing, and prepare reports on lists of
overdrawn accounts, loans in arrears on payments of principal, interest, and fees; requests for confirmation of deposit
balances by customers and third parties; outstanding loan
balances, collateral pledged, securities held in safekeeping,
and a multitude of other auditing inquiries. Thus the computer can take much of the drudgery out of many aspects of
auditing. It should be emphasized that data center operating
programs should not be used by the auditor to produce these
reports, listings, and confirmation requests, because if any-

one in the data center is engaged in fraud, theft, or embezzlement, he or she could very easily modify the print programs to suppress the printouts of those accounts in which the fraud or theft would be revealed.

Among other things, systems documentation includes the following:

1 A statement of the problem, or a detailed analysis of what was required from the new system to correct the inadequacies of the old system.

2 The feasibility study (including a preliminary systems design) that determined whether the function could be automated, whether it was advisable to do so, whether the estimated cost of building the system could be justified, and the estimated time frame in which it could be accomplished.

3 Official approval of the feasibility study, accompanied by authorization to proceed further with the design and development of the system.

4 A narrative description of the new system, including objectives and the input, processing, and output stages.

5 Flow charts of the new system, highlighting all the critical control points in each of the stages.

6 Systems specifications for the programmers.

7 Programming flow charts or block diagrams.

8 Program listings.

9 Testing data, or transactions, and the results.

10 A detailed description of the controls.

11 Layouts of all the system's records.

12 Layouts of all the new input and output forms and reports.

13 Operating instructions for the data-center operators and the operations users.

14   A copy of the final program used when the system "went operational."

15   Written official approval to stop running the old and new systems in parallel, that is, to drop the old system and make the new system the official operating system.

16   A record of all members of the project team, including the project manager, systems analysts, programmers, and user representatives such as operations personnel, account officers, auditing representatives, or anyone involved with input or output of the system.

17   A record of approved requests for changes to the system, accompanied by system and programming flow charts showing the changes and the controls affected. It should be a firm policy of the bank that no major changes be made to any system without the prior approval of the users, the auditor, and management.

Systems documentation should be prepared in duplicate sets, one for the computer systems department and one for the auditing department.

Participation by the internal auditor in the design, development, and implementation of an automated system not only gives the system every chance of being properly designed and controlled, but also saves the bank the additional cost of having to incorporate omitted controls or other specifications after the system is already running. It also protects the bank against loss, embarrassment, and probable liability, and should promote mutual understanding and respect among the technicians, users, and auditors.

The auditor's job is not finished when the system is complete and running. This system and all other automated systems, especially those that were designed and developed without audit participation, must continue to be reviewed and tested periodically. The auditor's responsibility is to make certain that all systems, both manual and automated, continue to operate efficiently, that their controls continue to be effective, that there is no unauthorized intervention in the processing, and that there are no changes to the systems without prior approval by the users, analysts, programmers, and the internal auditor. The systems documentation must also be reviewed from time to time to make sure that it has been kept up to date and reflects the details of all changes made since it first "went operational."

Periodic Audits of Automated Systems

There was a time when the internal bank auditor could audit computer systems without worrying about what went on inside "the big black box," or the central processing unit. The audit was accomplished by tracing initial input transactions, using the actual documents, through the computer processing maze by reviewing the computer printouts produced throughout the many processing stages. This was the approach in the early days of the computer because so many of the computer monitoring and control features had to be programmed, and printouts were almost automatically produced throughout the processing. Using this visible trail of printouts to audit a computer system is known as auditing around the computer. The auditor did not think it necessary to participate in the design and development of the systems, nor to inquire into the systems or controls. As long as the printouts gave the auditor visual assurance that transactions were correct and had reached their predetermined destinations, and the totals proved with the subsidiary and general ledger accounts, all was well. Auditors who persist in this attitude will soon be lost in the shuffle, if they are not already. Computers are now being built with so many of the necessary controls and data-monitoring and -operating systems already in place, that auditing around the computer will have to be discarded.

Auditing around the computer can still be done to a degree

where batch processing systems are involved. Batch processing systems are magnetic tape systems requiring sequential processing, that is, every transaction must be in order by account number or other numerical sequence, because magnetic tape systems do not lend themselves to random access processing. Batch systems process transactions after they have taken place, and usually involve high-volume functions. At the end of a business day, the transactions have to be batched and put into machine-readable form for processing. In some instances, they are received in machine-readable form, or at least partially so. For example, the printer encodes the account numbers on checks and deposit slips by Magnetic Ink Character Recognition (MICR), but of course the dollar amounts have to be encoded by hand-operated MICR-encoding machines. The batched transactions are then transferred to magnetic tape for speed in processing.

However, even where batch systems are concerned, auditing around the computer is not a very satisfactory approach. The engineering of modern computers and their peripheral hardware is most sophisticated and provides capabilities that ensure accuracy of processing unheard of in the past. For example, hardware controls built into the computer verify the computer's own computations and the validity of alphabetic and numeric characters in the computer core because they can lose magnetic bits as they are transferred from one area in the computer to another. The computer lets the operator know when something is wrong by using indicators or by bringing the processing to a halt. The read-and-write heads of a tape drive also perform a read-after-write check to make sure that data copied from the computer core onto tape have been copied correctly. These are just a few of the current built-in hardware controls, and more are coming. Together with a central processing unit that possesses no moving parts, these controls provide unbelievably reliable computer processing.

There are all types of programmed processing controls in the form of stored programs covering input, transmission of data, processing of data, and output that add still further to creating safe, accurate, and efficient systems. It is in this area that the internal auditor plays a most important role during the design and development stage.

There are also computer-generated entries such as the automatic computation of interest on deposits, fees, and commissions that are triggered by a computer calendar, computed, and posted to accounts automatically without any interference by operators or programmers. Of course, programs for these entries have to be written and imbedded in the main program, but once in place, they may be forgotten. Correctly instructed, the computer will perform without error unless it is disrupted by outside interference.

The computer is unbelievably fast, operating in billionths of a second, too fast for the mind to visualize but making it possible to process more than one system at a time. Multiprocessing is commonplace. Everything seems to be happening at once, but the processing actually is sequential. It is the fantastic speed that makes it seem to be taking place at the same time.

Under conditions such as these, and considering the tremendous cost involved, printouts of what is happening inside the computer will only add to the cost and time required, thus defeating the original purpose of automating systems.

There are also on-line, real-time systems that are random access systems. Transactions and master files do not have to be in sequence. The input and output appear to occur together, because transactions are processed as they take place. Magnetic disk packs instead of tape are used, and accounts can be accessed almost instantaneously and posted immediately. Controls for these systems are also critical because they are very vulnerable to unauthorized, outside interference. Almost everyone has had some contact with these systems. Airline ticket agents use them to book passenger space, and savings bank tellers as well as commercial bank tellers use them via terminal to instantly record customers' deposits and withdrawals. They can also use the terminals to retrieve a customer's balance from the disk files and find out whether a check has been paid or a deposit collected.

The most effective way of auditing these systems is to use the computer to test the systems by passing test transactions through dummy files or copies of the files. The auditor must extract the information needed with computer auditing programs prepared either by an electronic data processing auditor or by an outside consultant or technician. If the internal bank auditor can do the programming, so much the better for the bank. Programs can be written to compare the program in use when the system "went operational" with the program currently being used in the data center. In this way, as the exceptions are printed out, the auditor can find any unauthorized changes or impairment of controls that could be part of an ongoing fraud or embezzlement. Computer programs are available commercially to do all kinds of testing and to prepare many types of reports. The computer takes the drudgery out of auditing and leaves the auditor more time to analyze and do a more thorough job. It should be emphasized again that computer auditing programs must not be prepared by anyone in the computer systems department, because anyone in that area could be acting in collusion with someone in the data center or elsewhere to divert funds from customers' accounts or from the bank's income accounts to accounts fraudulently set up by the perpetrators.

Auditing the Data Center Operations

It is in the data center that familiar internal controls known as segregation of duties, dual control, mandatory vacations, and rotation of employees are extremely valuable and should be enforced without exception. This is an operating area established simply to process the work of the bank on automated systems. It is an extremely vulnerable area because many computer operators are also programmers (although they might keep it under wraps) and can therefore make unauthorized changes to systems for their own advantage and perhaps also for accomplices. The data center should be totally separated from the rest of the computer systems department; systems analysts and application programmers should not be permitted access except for testing purposes, and then under strict control or supervision. The following official rules should be enforced:

1   Systems analysts and application programmers should not be permitted to substitute for regular computer operators to carry out the daily processing runs.

2   Data center operators should not be allowed to prepare input to the systems, initiate changes in the input received, or verify the controls or output.

3   Data center computer operators should be required to take at least two consecutive weeks of vacation away from the bank.

4   There should be frequent rotation of computer operators so that no one operator is allowed to process the same daily runs for too long a period of time.

5   There should be an independent control person or persons to verify the daily control proofs, review the output for reasonableness and obvious errors, make certain that all reports scheduled to be prepared have been prepared and distributed to the proper people, that exceptions and errors recorded on the console typewriter are followed up for resolution and correction, and that all entries into the system through the console are investigated thoroughly.

Security of Tape and Disk Files

All master tape and disk files should be housed in a computer library under the control of a librarian and released only to operators designated to use them for processing the day's work. Care should be taken that they are returned to the library at the end of the runs.

There should be external file labels on all files as well as internal labels on tapes and disks and file protection rings placed on all tapes that are to be retained in the library.

All files should have backup protection in the form of duplicates housed either off the premises under security or in another part of the building that is properly air-conditioned and secured. Provision should also be made for reconstruction of files in the event of fire or other damage. This can be done by retaining the previous day's master files and transaction tapes.

Access to the data center must be restricted to data center employees, who should be provided with identification cards. Visitors should be identified and accompanied at all times by an officer of the data center.

Entrances and exits should be guarded and locked at all times.

Bank Security and Protection

Hardly a week goes by that newspapers and news broadcasts do not tell about law enforcement officers, bank guards, bank managers and employees, and others being cut down or threatened with bodily harm by armed robbers, burglers, terrorists, kidnappers, and other assorted criminals. Certainly, the public must wonder what banks are doing to protect their premises, their assets, their customers' property, their employees, and of course members of the general public who might be on the scene at the wrong time. There must also be some question about what the law requires that banks do to protect themselves and the public, but it is doubtful whether the role of the auditor in this specialized protection is ever questioned by the average person or even by banking customers.

Bank management, specifically the Board of Directors, has always been responsible for the safety of the bank's assets, the property of customers left in its care, its employees, and members of the general public who find themselves on the premises when trouble erupts. How banks have gone about providing this protection is another matter.

Armed guards have always been a vital part of the protection provided. Traditionally, security and protection were also among the primary concerns of the internal bank auditor, who until about 1968 was actively involved in providing this protection. Much of what the auditor did and recommended in the past is still being done today, but in conjunction with a specialist in security and protection. There was, however, no definitive legislation setting forth specific protective requirements for banks to follow. There was only legislation for the punishment of criminals who were caught and convicted. There was, though, a considerable amount of self-help provided within the banking industry by organizations such as the American Bankers Association and the Bank Administration Institute, formerly known as the National Association of Bank Auditors and Controllers (NABAC) and founded in 1924. These were and still are the largest and best-known associations of bankers in the country and the most influential. There are of course many state bankers associations, both commercial and savings, that have been making substantial contributions to the effort, as well as the many law enforcement agencies, in particular the Federal Bureau of Investigation (FBI). It should be noted that during the past several years, the FBI has been extremely concerned not only about armed robbery, kidnapping, and other forms of violent crimes against banks, but also about the more insidious white-collar fraud within the industry. They have been bringing in their experienced agents from the field for intensive training and seminars on the subject of internal bank fraud. Although successful perpetrators of internal fraud normally do not resort to violence, they might conceivably be connected with armed robberies or other crimes of force.

It wasn't until July of 1968 that Congress, aroused by the unprecedented increase in crimes against banks, passed the Bank Protection Act. This legislation charged the various regulatory bodies with responsibility for establishing comprehensive and definitive security requirements for banks to follow and for setting and enforcing strict compliance and reporting requirements.

Early in 1969, the major federal regulatory agencies, that is, the Comptroller of the Currency, the Federal Deposit Insurance Corporation, and the Federal Reserve Bank, published their requirements and standards for security and protection in banks under their jurisdiction and set dates for compliance and reporting. (See Comptroller of the Currency 12 CFR 21 and Regulation P of the Board of Governors of the Federal Reserve System). Regulation P covers state member banks of the Federal Reserve System.

These regulations are so broad in scope and so specific in their requirements that it is not hard to understand why internal bank auditors could not possibly assume full responsibility for their implementation and enforcement. As a matter of fact, the regulations are quite specific in requiring that bank boards of directors appoint a knowledgeable and competent officer or other employee to take full charge of the security and protection program and consult with law enforcement agencies in the development and implementation of their programs. In many large- and medium-sized banks, the boards have appointed former law enforcement officers to assume this responsibility. The present legal, social, and economic environment presents problems of such complexity and sensitivity that specialized expertise must be brought in to cope with them.

The internal bank auditor continues to be deeply concerned and rightly so, particularly if the auditor is what an auditor should be, a strong, knowledgeable generalist in the subject matter of banking and especially in the operations of his or her own bank as well as a competent, alert auditor. The auditor remains responsible for making certain that all vulnerable areas of operations, administration, and management are protected as effectively as possible against all types of threats. It is not always possible to anticipate the occurrence of some threats. A kidnapping, for example, cannot be anticipated in most instances unless there has been some advance warning, a phone call or a note stating that it will take place. All that can be done is to prepare in advance a course of action to be followed in the event that such a catastrophe should occur. The internal auditor must maintain close communication with the security officer appointed by the board and periodically review and appraise the program of security and protection, the manner in which it is being carried out and the degree to which the staff as a whole is complying with it. It should be remembered that the auditor and auditing staff have a unique opportunity to observe what is going on throughout the bank, and their observations might very well be the means by which the security officer can either prevent or close in on a plan of action against the bank, its officers, and its employees.

Just as the purpose of this book is not to make an internal bank auditor of the reader, but simply to clarify and make understandable the philosophy, principles, and techniques of the profession as well as the scope of the bank auditing problem, so the purpose of this chapter must of necessity be equally modest. It is to make the reader aware of the complexity and enormity of the task of securing and protecting a bank and to define the role of the internal bank auditor in that undertaking.

SCOPE OF SECURITY AND PROTECTIVE REQUIREMENTS

Cash

Hard, cold cash is, of course, the loot most desired by robbers, burglars, extortionists, and others. As everyone knows, cash is held in the tellers' positions on the main banking floor in limited amounts. Larger cash reserves are held in the vault. Cash is found in many other places as well. Banking floors where the officers and tellers are usually located are open to the public and filled with customers ready to make deposits or cash checks; they may also have on their persons jewels or other items of value such as credit cards, securities, and the like. Cash is also deposited in night depositories and pours into and out of cash receiving and dispensing machines. Coin and currency are always being shipped into and out of banks for one reason or another, such as deliveries from the Federal Reserve Bank, payroll shipments to customers, and so forth. What kind of protection is effective in these situations, or is there any?

Securities

Stocks, bonds, and other items of value are also to be found in many other areas of the bank. Obviously, securities entrusted by customers to the bank's care or held by the bank as executor and/or trustee as well as securities belonging to the bank's own portfolio are held in the bank's vault under tight control. But these same securities are not static. They are always in the process of being bought, sold, redeemed, exchanged, or delivered free to customers, beneficiaries, and remaindermen, or to charities, foundations, and relatives as gifts or for various other reasons. This processing of securities transactions is a complicated and extended operation. The securities pass through many hands within the bank and outside of the bank. Unfortunately, because of the need to maintain public confidence in the banking industry, the responsibility for their safety remains with the banks in spite of the fact that many times loss occurs when the securities are in the hands of others.

Securities are also to be found in a branch's general cage, which is usually on the banking floor near the tellers and open to the general public. Customers bring the securities in because they have sold them and want the bank to deliver them to the broker on the settlement date and collect the proceeds of sale for credit to the customers' accounts. Or the customer might simply have brought them in for deposit in the customer's custodian account. Branch offices also often carry large supplies of unissued savings bonds.

Corporate Trust Departments of large commercial banks often act as stock transfer agents and dividend disbursing agents for corporations whose stocks are listed and traded on the exchanges. This means that when shares of these stocks are bought and sold they are sent to the transfer agents to be debited and credited to the old and new owners' accounts. The shares sold are cancelled and new certificates are issued to the new owners. Since these transfer agents maintain the shareholder records for the corporations involved, they also pay out the declared dividends to the shareholders of record. It is therefore necessary for Corporate Trust Departments to carry large amounts of unissued stock and sometimes also bond certificates, which can represent substantial value.

In large commercial banks, particularly in money market centers such as New York, there are brokers' loan departments that finance the heavy trading liabilities of the better-known brokers and investment banking firms. For the most part, these loans are secured by the brokers with their "grade A" securities. Because of time restrictions and as a matter of convenience, these securities are not held in the banks' vaults during business hours. Brokers frequently find it necessary to withdraw securities to meet trading commitments and to substitute others. They might also want to pay off their loans in full and retrieve their collateral. In this type of business there is no time to comply with most bank's strict vault deposit and withdrawal procedures; the brokers' deadlines would never be met. The securities therefore are held in fire-resistant, movable safes on the floors of the Brokers' Loan Departments so that securities held as collateral may be withdrawn and delivered at a moment's notice. Although these areas are secured and guarded, messengers carrying securities, checks, and documents of importance must have immediate access and therein lies the weakness. How is one to know who is a messenger and who is not? Of course, after business hours, these movable safes are locked under the control of the Brokers' Loan Department and rolled, presumably through secured routes, into the vault.

The same situation exists in large commercial loan departments and in branches. Securities held as collateral for secured loans must be readily available for substitution or withdrawal or for delivery in the event of payment of the loan.

Computer Centers and Magnetic Tape and Disk Libraries

Banking operations today are highly automated, and the data processing and file storage areas are very vulnerable unless they are tightly controlled and protected. Even then, banks face disaster from internal sabotage. In the data processing centers where the computers are housed and in the magnetic tape and disk libraries reside the vital official records of property belonging to bank customers, records of the banks assets and liabilities, employee records, and miscellaneous other but nevertheless important records without which the bank would be in deep trouble. These records are recorded on magnetic tape, disks, and punched cards in machine language and can be erased—wiped out in a flash—by disgruntled employees, assorted other criminals, fire, explosion, and water damage. It is generally acknowledged that most computer crimes are perpetrated through the computer by accessing the data base or by changing the operating or application software. In other words, criminals can obtain information to which they have no right or can change instruction programs to manipulate data to the detriment of others. A fine line divides responsibility for this type of crime between the security officer, who should be involved, and the internal bank auditor. Responsibility for apprehending and convicting the criminals rests with the security officer, but the internal auditor is responsible for appraising the physical security of the data center and tape and disk libraries as well as for reviewing and evaluating the adequacy and safety of the data bases and the computer operating and application software. Such reviews and evaluations if professionally carried out should disclose or hopefully prevent destruction of files and fraudulent operations. Thus the auditor's responsibility in an automated environment is no different than in a nonautomated environment.

On-line, real-time systems are more vulnerable because terminals are used through which data bases and software can be more readily accessed. These terminals are usually located on banking premises, but there is a growing trend toward placing them in the offices of customers, their agents, and agents of the bank. For example, banks sell cash management services to corporations, and employee benefit departments sell portfolio and investment advisory services to pension trust customers. Both of these services if they are competitive require the use of terminals by the customers and their agents. Remotely located terminals present a danger that must be dealt with in the near future. In-house terminals are also a danger, but should be easier to control, whereas remote terminals are in reality out of the bank's control.

Safe Deposit Vaults

The rental of safe deposit boxes is surely not one of the big money earning services of a bank; it is more in the nature of a public service. When the risks involved are taken into consideration, it is a wonder that any bank would even contemplate offering the service. The contents of a safe deposit box should be known only to the customer or lessee, which makes it very difficult for the bank if the customer claims that something is missing. The bank is in an even worse position if the safe deposit vault is burglarized and the lessees file very large loss claims. Who knows if the customers are telling the truth? In the first instance, if the customer claims that something is missing, the bank will be in a good position if it can prove that its procedures for renting and permitting access to safe deposit boxes are prudent and enforced, and that no person other than the lessee or an authorized deputy ever had access to the box. The burden of proof then is on the lessee. If, on the other hand, the safe deposit vault was burglarized, the bank cannot resort to proof of prudent practice. The bank's position becomes even worse if the lessee can prove ownership of the missing items and further, that it was the customer's practice to put them in the safe deposit box. There are, of course, many rules of evidence and legal procedures that cannot be addressed here. It is obvious, however, that the bank must be able to prove the following:

1 That bank rules and regulations governing the rental of safe deposit boxes and access to them are adequate, prudent, and enforced.
2 That proper security measures such as armed guards, locked gates, alarms, surveillance cameras, and so forth are provided.

Safety of the Premises

This problem will confound even the most knowledgeable and experienced security officer. It not only requires that officers know intimately every detail of the physical layout of each floor, but that they be able to determine what restrictions should be and, from a practical point of view, can be imposed against access to each area. The departments and divisions engaged primarily in critical banking operations should be totally secured; that is, access should be restricted to those employees with official identity cards, and all others desiring access should be properly identified, vouched for, and permitted entry only in the company of an officer or designated employee of that department or division.

There are other areas of the banking premises which are and must be public areas, or if not totally public, then controlled and monitored in some way. This problem becomes a bit more complicated when part of the bank building is leased to outsiders, or when the bank is renting the part in which it conducts business. People working for or calling on tenants cannot be prevented from entering certain areas during business hours, and it is this particular reality that poses the greatest danger to the banking areas. A partial list of such areas would include the following:

Lobbies
Corridors
Elevators
Stairwells
Reception areas
Wash rooms not restricted to bank employees
Service and delivery entrances

Safety of Personnel

The greatest concern of any organization and especially a bank should be the safety of its staff, both official and nonofficial. The basic, underlying theme of any program of security and protection, therefore, should be the inculcation of an awareness of danger and how to protect oneself against it. It doesn't take too much imagination to realize that if employees can mobilize their forces to protect themselves, they are in a much better position to protect the bank.

The following is a list of threats to which banks, bank executives, and personnel may be exposed:

Armed robbery
Bomb threats
Extortion
Kidnapped or taken hostage
Burglary
Crank callers

Nature of Protection

Bankwide security is really a bankwide personnel problem. It is not just a matter of armed guards, surveillance cameras, alarms, vaults, and other devices. It is a bankwide state of mind created by a practical, well-constructed program of security and protection. It must include a comprehensive training program for all employees, tellers, vault officers, managers, guards, the clerical staff, specialists, and employees in all departments, as well as all officers and top management. The training required for each category of personnel will of necessity incorporate different perspectives, different perceptions, and different techniques, but it must universally stress alertness to danger signals and the urgent need for constant vigilance. This type of training is not a one-time thing but a continuing effort. Total security, in spite of everyone's best efforts, is not a reasonably attainable goal under today's conditions, nor has it ever been within the memory of man, but much can be done to prevent and minimize the effects of many types of crime. There is no substitute for prudence and no excuse for not exercising it; in fact, failure to do so may result in both loss of insurance and formidable legal liability.

Protective Measures

Areas where cash, securities, and other items of value are housed or processed should be equipped with armed guards, at least in the opinion of the writer. There are those who would take issue with this statement, but it might be difficult to deny the value of well-trained, alert, crack shots on a main banking floor when an armed robbery is taking place or when the security of a vault is being threatened. These areas should be made as secure as possible. Access to vaults, tellers' cages, computer centers, securities handling areas, and other areas should be rigidly restricted to those who work there and are properly identified as employees of those areas. Tellers' areas of course are open to the public, but the inner cages themselves must be restricted to the tellers, clerks, and managers. They must be kept locked and the counters kept as free as possible of cash and other items of value. The counters themselves should be so constructed that it would be difficult for a thief or robber to reach over and scoop up cash, or perhaps even to vault over, which has frequently happened. The friendly bank atmosphere that management has tried to create by installing low counters is disappearing. Surveillance cameras and alarms are of course a must, but personnel needs to be instructed in how to activate these devices without attracting the attention of the criminals.

Training programs should include instructions in what to do before, during, and after a holdup, kidnapping, bomb threat, and so forth. Personnel should be taught how to protect themselves at the bank, at home, and on the streets, how to spot suspicious individuals, and how to be noncommunicative about the bank and its affairs, its protection and security devices, and its people. Every employee should be provided with emergency phone numbers, names of people to contact, and procedures to follow in an emergency.

Security and protection for the bank and its officers and employees is a round-the-clock undertaking both inside and outside of the bank, and this should be made clear to everyone. Training should include acting out mock holdups, kidnappings, and other threats, with emphasis on self-protection and the need to keep calm, alert, and observant. The accuracy with which details about the event, the criminals, and others can be recalled and reported to law enforcement officers will greatly aid in the ultimate identification, apprehension, and conviction of the criminals.

Applicable Banking Laws and Regulations

This book is concerned exclusively with the subject of internal auditing of commercial banks, how it serves management and provides protection for management, stockholders, depositors, and other customers. Part of that protection is the ongoing determination by the internal auditor that there has been and continues to be compliance by management and operations with the applicable banking laws and regulations. This is no easy task; the laws are complex, the regulations are even worse, and there are always the overriding decisions by the higher courts which in effect construe the statutes and regulations and have the effect of statutory law. Internal auditors must always be aware that there is much they do not know and must therefore consult with bank counsel at all times. The secret is to recognize what you don't know and know where to get the information that is needed.

Commercial banks conduct business under a dual system of laws and regulations and miraculously do so successfully, although many times under great stress. A good number of commercial banks in the United States are national banks, chartered by the Comptroller of the Currency, who is in charge of a special division in the Department of the Treasury and who reports to the Secretary of the Treasury. The Comptroller of the Currency is also responsible for the supervision and examination of all national banks. The office of the Comptroller of the Currency was established in 1863 and although the Federal Reserve System has general jurisdiction over all banking in the United States and could theoretically also examine national banks, it studiously avoids that duplication of effort and instead accepts for review the examination reports provided by the Comptroller's Chief District Examiners covering examinations of the national banks in each district. National banks must become members of the Federal Reserve System and the Federal Deposit Insurance Corporation.

State banks are chartered by their respective state banking departments and may voluntarily become members of the Federal Reserve System. If they choose to do so, they must also become members of the Federal Deposit Insurance Corporation. Many state banks are members of the Federal Reserve System because of the many operating advantages available to members, even though they must set aside reserve balances with the Federal Reserve Bank in their district. Obviously, most state banks also want to become members of the Federal Deposit Insurance Corporation because of the public confidence generated by its insuring of customers' deposits.

State banks that are members of the Federal Reserve System and therefore also of the Federal Deposit Insurance Corporation are subject to examination by their respective state banking departments, the Federal Reserve System, and the Federal Deposit Insurance Corporation. Examination by three separate agencies can be quite a burden to the banks involved. Whenever possible, however, it is the policy of the federal reserve bank-examination departments to conduct joint examinations with state bank examiners or to alternate with them. This cooperative effort does lessen the burden.

The Federal Reserve System came into being when the Federal Reserve Act was signed by President Wilson on December 23, 1913. It was subsequently amended and enhanced substantially by the Banking Acts of 1933 and 1935. There have of course been many amendments since then as well as many other statutes passed by Congress which affect the Federal Reserve System. It is in effect the central banking system of the United States and its main purpose is to regulate the country's money supply, hopefully offsetting the detrimental effects of inflation and deflation. Another equally important mission of the Federal Reserve System is to supervise the banking system of the United States, in particular, state banks that are members of the Federal Reserve System.

In carrying out their official duties, the successive Comptrollers of the Currency and Boards of Governors of the Federal Reserve System have over the years contributed to an overwhelming body of rules and regulations with which every national and federal reserve bank examiner must be thoroughly familiar. Internal bank auditors and bank management should also familiarize themselves with this body of laws, rules, and regulations. They are the tools employed by the Comptroller of the Currency and the Federal Reserve System to help the banking industry execute all banking and related laws passed by Congress. A list of some of these laws and regulations follows.

Banking Act of 1933, which established the Federal Deposit Insurance Corporation

Banking Act of 1935

Bank Protection Act of 1968

Bank Secrecy Act

Civil Rights Act of 1964

Comptroller of the Currency's Code of Federal Regulations (CFR)

Comptroller of the Currency's Regulation 9: Fiduciary Powers of National Banks and Collective Investment Funds

Federal Deposit Insurance Corporation's rules and regulations

Federal Reserve regulations

Occupational Safety and Health Act of 1970

Penal Code

State commercial and savings bank laws, rules, and regulations

State trust and estate laws

State unclaimed property and escheat laws

State usury laws

The Employee Retirement Income Security Act (ERISA), passed in 1974

The Securities Act of 1933

The Securities and Exchange Act of 1934

The Securities Act Amendments of 1975

The Trust Indenture Act of 1939

The Uniform Commercial Code

U.S. Code

APPENDIX B

Comptroller of The Currency Comptroller's Handbook for National Bank Examiners

COMMERCIAL — INTERNATIONAL

INTERNAL CONTROL

Section 001.1

INTRODUCTION

This section sets forth the principal aspects of effective internal control and discusses some pertinent points to be considered in the completion of the standardized Internal Control Questionnaire. Although, in a broad sense, internal control includes the program of internal audit (where applicable), this section applies to the review and evaluation by bank examiners of the existing internal control within a bank. A separate handbook section addresses the topic of a bank's program of internal audit. However, the examiner should consider reviewing the program of internal audit activities in conjunction with the review of internal control because often useful information, such as system descriptions and procedures, can be extracted from internal audit working papers.

In a special report on internal control issued by the American Institute of Certified Public Accountants (AICPA) Committee on Working Procedures in 1949, a broad definition of internal control was established:

> Internal control comprises the plan of organization and all of the coordinate methods and measures adopted within the business to safeguard its assets, check the accuracy and reliability of its accounting data, promote operational efficiency, and encourage adherence to subscribed managerial policies. This definition possibly is broader than the meaning sometimes attributed to the term. It recognizes that "system" of internal control extends beyond those matters which relate directly to the functions of the accounting and financial departments. Such a system might include budgetary control, standard costs, periodic operating reports, statistical analyses and dissemination thereof, a training program designed to aid personnel in meeting their responsibilities, and an internal audit staff to provide additional assurance to management as to the adequacy of its outlined procedures and the extent to which they are being effectively carried out . . .

That broad definition is a clear indication that development and maintenance of a satisfactory system of internal control is a managerial responsibility within a bank.

A later definition by the AICPA divided internal control into two components:

Administrative control includes, but is not limited to, the plan of organization and the procedures and records that are concerned with the decision processes leading to management's authorization of transactions.* Such authorization is a management function directly associated with the responsibility for achieving the objectives of the organization and is the starting point for establishing accounting control of transactions.

Accounting control comprises the plan of organization and the procedures and records that are concerned with the safeguarding of assets and the reliability of financial records and consequently are designed to provide reasonable assurance that:

    a Transactions are executed in accordance with management's general or specific authorization.

    b Transactions are recorded as necessary
        (1) to permit preparation of financial statements in conformity with generally accepted accounting principles or any other criteria applicable to such statements and
        (2) to maintain accountability for assets.

    c Access to assets is permitted only in accordance with management's authorization.

    d The recorded accountability for assets is compared with the existing assets at reasonable intervals and appropriate action is taken with respect to any differences.

---

*This definition is intended only to provide a point of departure for distinguishing accounting control, and consequently, is not necessarily definitive for other purposes.

The foregoing definitions are not necessarily mutually exclusive because some of the procedures and records comprehended in accounting control may also be involved in administrative control.*

Although much of the remainder of this section is devoted to a discussion of accounting control and the evaluation of such control, the internal control portions of the other sections also include many questions concerned primarily with the evaluation of a bank's policies, practices and procedures (described above as Administrative Controls). The concept of operational efficiency and the related administrative controls have not been included herein because the OCC believes that such considerations generally fall outside the responsibilities of a national bank examiner. That, however, is not intended to inhibit or prevent an examiner from commenting on operational inefficiencies, particularly in instances where inefficiencies have a significant impact on the condition of a bank.

OBJECTIVES

In general, "good" internal control exists when no one person is in a position to make significant errors or perpetrate significant irregularities without timely detection. Therefore, a system of internal control should include those procedures necessary to assure timely detection of a failure of accountability, and such procedures should be performed by competent persons who have no incompatible duties. The following requirements are encompassed within the foregoing description of internal control:

Existence of Procedures   Existence of prescribed internal control procedures is necessary but not sufficient for effective internal control. For example, prescribed procedures

*Statement on Auditing Standards 1, American Institute of Certified Public Accountants.

that are not performed do nothing to establish control. Consequently the examiner must give thoughtful attention, not only to the prescribed set of procedures, but also to the practices actually followed. That can be accomplished through inquiry, observation, testing, or a combination thereof. The responsibility for determining the existence of procedures rests with each member of the examination staff and is not restricted to the examiner-in-charge. Assisting personnel cannot perform their duties properly without understanding a bank's procedures applicable to each area of the examination and the resultant impact of those procedures on the evaluation of existing internal control. Also, assisting personnel may be the only persons who know if the controls are effective, because they test the documentary support or observe the actual practices within a given department at the time other examination procedures are performed.

Competent Performance   For internal control to be effective, the required procedures must be performed by competent persons. Evaluation of competence undoubtedly requires some degree of subjective judgment because attributes such as intelligence, knowledge, and attitude are relevant. Thus, the examiner should be alert for indications that employees have failed so substantially to perform their duties that a serious question is raised concerning their abilities.

Independent Performance   If an employee, who is accountable for assets or other valuables, or who performs duties significant in the internal control system, is permitted to avoid the established controls by reason of the performance of other assigned tasks, the individual has incompatible duties and the control is thereby weakened. If employees who have access to assets also have access to the related accounting records or also perform related review operations (or immediately supervise the activities of other employees who maintain the records or perform the review operations), they may be able both to perpetrate and to conceal defalcations. Therefore, duties concerned with the custody of assets are incompatible with recordkeeping duties for those assets, and duties concerned with the performance of activities are incompatible with the authorization or review of those activities. In judging the independence of a person, the examiner must avoid looking at that person as an individual and presuming the way in which he or she would respond in a given situation. For example, a cashier may be the sole check signer and an assistant may prepare the monthly bank reconcilement; these are different people and, if the assistant appears to be a competent person, it may seem that an independent reconcilement would be performed and anything amiss would be reported, even though the assistant is under the direct supervision of the cashier. Such judgments are potentially erroneous. There exists no established tests by which the psychological and economic independence of an individual in a given situation can be judged. The position must be evaluated, not the person. If the position in which the person acts is not an independent one in itself, then the work should not be presumed to be independent regardless of the apparent competence of the persons in question. In the example cited above, the function performed by the assistant should be viewed as if it were performed by the cashier. Hence, incompatible duties are present in that situation.

PROCEDURES

The OCC's Internal Control Questionnaire, which is composed of internal control questions from the various sections of the handbook, provides a basis for determining the bank's control procedures. To reach conclusions required by the questionnaire, the examiner assigned to review a given internal control routine or area of bank operations should utilize any source of information necessary to insure a full understanding of the prescribed system, including any potential weaknesses. Only when the examiner completely understands the bank's system can an assessment and evaluation be made of the effects of internal controls on the examination.

In obtaining and substantiating the answers to the questions contained in the Internal Control Questionnaire, the examiner should develop a plan to obtain the necessary information in the most efficient manner. Such a plan would normally avoid a direct question and answer session with bank officers, primarily because of the excessive time required. A suggested approach to completion of the Internal Control Questionnaire is to:

Become familiar with the questionnaire.

Review any written documentation of bank's system of controls.

Find out what the department head does and the functions of personnel within the department through conversations with appropriate individuals.

Answer as many individual questions as possible from information gained in the preceding steps and fill in the remaining questions by direct inquiry.

Substantiate questions during the course of the examination, rather than as a specially designed task.

Set out to specifically substantiate those significant answers which have not been substantiated only after examination procedures have been completed.

To reach conclusions concerning a specific section of the questionnaire, the examiner should document and review the bank's operating systems and procedures by consulting all available sources of information and by discussing such with appropriate bank personnel. Sources of information might include organization charts, procedural manuals, operating instructions, job specifications, directives to employees, and other similar sources of information. Also, the examiner should not overlook potential sources such as job descriptions, flowcharts and other documentation contained in internal audit working papers. A primary objective in the review of the system is to efficiently reach a conclusion about the overall adequacy of existing controls. Any existing source of information which will enable the examiner to quickly gain an understanding of the procedures in effect should be used in order to minimize the time required to formulate the conclusions. The review should be documented in an organized manner through the use of narrative descriptions, flowcharts or other diagrams. Any readily available information, such as system flowcharts or job procedure descriptions, should be reproduced or excerpted and incorporated to avoid duplication of effort.

Supporting documentation should be referenced and filed with the Internal Control Questionnaire in the working papers. The complete documentation of a system is important because it facilitates an efficient review and provides a written basis for the examiner's conclusions about the adequacy of internal controls. If a system is properly documented, the documentation will provide a ready reference for any examiner performing work in the area and often it may be carried forward for future examinations, thereby effecting huge time savings.

Although narrative descriptions can often provide an adequate explanation of systems of internal control, especially in less complex situations, they may have certain drawbacks, such as:

They may be cumbersome; often lengthy narratives result.
They may not be clear; narratives may be poorly written.
Related points may be difficult to integrate.
Annual changes may be awkward to record.

To overcome these problems the examiner should consider using flowcharts, which, in essence, reduce narrative descriptions to a picture. Flowcharts are useful tools and often reduce a complex situation to an easily understandable sequence of interrelated steps.

The Internal Control Questionnaire has been designed so that a "no" answer discloses the possibility of an internal control weakness. However, evaluating internal control requires alertness, imagination and understanding on the part of the examiner. Hence, the emphasis should be on an overall indication of weakness in a given area or section of a bank's operations and a few negative answers will not necessarily be indicative of an overall deficiency in internal control. Explanations of "no" answers may be appropriate and should include a statement that either no weaknesses exist because of alternative controls or a weakness exists because compensating internal controls are absent. Also, a combination of negative answers may indicate that a serious deficiency in internal control exists in a particular area or operation of a bank. Accordingly, the examiner should carefully consider the overall impact of all negative answers in evaluating the effectiveness of internal controls in each area of the bank.

An effective way to begin a review of internal control is to identify the various key functions applicable to the area under review. For each position identified, the following questions should then be asked:

Is this a critical position? That is, can a person in this position either make a significant error that will affect the recording of transactions or perpetrate material irregularities of some type?

If an error is made or irregularity perpetrated, what is the probability that normal routines will disclose it on a timely basis? That is, what controls exist that would prevent or detect significant errors or the perpetration of significant irregularities?

What are the specific opportunities open to the individual to conceal any irregularity, and are there any mitigating controls that will reduce or eliminate these opportunities?

Although all employees within an organization may be subject to control, not all have financial responsibilities that can influence the accuracy of the accounting and financial records, or have authorized access to assets. It is those positions with ability to influence the records and with access to assets with which the examiner is primarily concerned. Once those positions have been identified, the examiners must exercise their professional knowledge of bank operations to visualize the possibilities open to any person holding a particular position. The question is not whether the individual is honest, but rather whether situations exist that might permit an error to be concealed. By directing attention to such situations, an examiner will also consider situations that may permit unintentional errors to remain undetected.

A question near the end of each section of the questionnaire concerns other circumstances that impair any controls or mitigate any weaknesses indicated by answers to the preceding questions. Thus, before an apparent weakness or established control is accepted, the evaluation of internal control should include consideration of other existing accounting and administrative controls or other circumstances that might counteract or mitigate an apparent weakness or impair an established control. Controls which mitigate an apparent weakness may be a formal part of the bank's operating system, such as budget procedures that include a careful comparison of budgeted and actual amounts by competent management personnel. Mitigating controls may also be informal. For example, in small banks, management may be sufficiently involved in daily operations to know the purpose and reasonableness of all expense disbursements. That knowledge, coupled with the responsibility for signing checks, may make irregularities by non-management personnel unlikely, even if disbursements are otherwise under the control of only one person.

When reviewing internal controls, an essential part of the examination is an alertness to indications that adverse circumstances may exist. Adverse circumstances may lead employees or officers into courses of action they normally would not pursue. An adverse circumstance to which the examiner should be especially alert exists when the personal financial interests of key officers or employees depend directly on operating results or financial condition. Although the review of internal control does not place the examiner in the role of an investigator or detective, an alert attitude toward possible conflicts of interest should be maintained throughout the examination. Also, offices staffed by members of the same family, branches completely dominated by a strong personality, or departments in which supervisors rely unduly on their assistants require special alertness on the part of the examiner. Those circumstances and other similar ones should be considered in preparing the questionnaire. It is not the formality of the particular factor that is of importance, but rather its effect on the overall operation under review. When circumstances that may affect answers to the basic questions exist, a notation of them should be made with conclusions concerning their impact on the examination.

The questionnaire was designed so that answers could be substantiated by inquiry to bank personnel, by observation, or by test. However, certain questions are marked with asterisks to indicate that they require substantiation through observation or testing. Those questions are deemed so critical that substantiation by inquiry is not sufficient. For those questions substantiated through testing, the nature and extent of the test performed should be indicated adjacent to the applicable step in the questionnaire.

The examiner should be alert for deviations by bank personnel from established policies, practices and procedures. That applies not only to questions marked with asterisks, but also to every question in the questionnaire. Examples of such deviations include situations when: instructions and directives are frequently not revised to reflect current practices; employees find "short cuts" for performing their tasks; changes in organization and activities may influence operating procedures in unexpected ways; employees' duties may be rotated in ways that have not been previously considered. Those and other circumstances may serve to modify or otherwise change prescribed procedures and so the examiner has an inadequate basis for evaluating internal control until the practices actually in effect are determined. Assisting personnel should report any deviations from prescribed procedures promptly, including an evaluation of the importance of the deviations. The examiner-in-charge then should determine their overall significance to the procedures to be performed.

Sometimes, when a substantial portion of the accounting work is accomplished by computer, the procedures are so different from conventional accounting methods that the principles discussed herein seem inapplicable. Care should be taken to resist that feeling. This discussion of internal control and its evaluation is purposely stated in terms sufficiently general to apply to any system. Perpetration of defalcations requires direct or indirect access to appropriate documents or accounting records. As such, perpetration requires the involvement of people and, under any system, computerized or not, there will be persons who have access to assets and to records. Those with access may include computer operators, programmers, their supervisors, and others and, under those circumstances, concealment may require somewhat different detailed steps; the basic requirements for perpetration and concealment are identical. The OCC also has developed an Internal Control Questionnaire for electronic data processing systems that is included in the work program utilized by its EDP examiners.

The final question in each section of the questionnaire requires a composite evaluation of existing internal controls in the applicable area of the bank. The examiner should base that evaluation on answers to the preceding questions within the section, on the review and observation of the systems and controls within the bank and on discussions with appropriate bank personnel. The composite evaluation of internal control should be designated as "good," "medium" or "bad." That evaluation relates to the minimum extent of testing considered appropriate in each area of the examination. In many cases the prescribed internal controls will be such that the predominance of questions will be answered either yes or no, thereby clearly indicating the overall effectiveness of internal controls as either "good" or "bad." When there is no predominance of yes or no answers, the examiner might weigh all factors and decide, as a practical matter, to use the "medium" evaluation.

The composite evaluation does, however, require some degree of subjective judgment. Thus, no strict criteria exist which delineate the three evaluations of internal control. Instead, the examiner should utilize all information available to formulate an overall evaluation, fully realizing that a high degree of professional judgment is required. In cases where the examiner is uncertain between two evaluations of the effectiveness of internal controls within a section of a bank, the least effective evaluation should be used. Also, if statistical sampling is to be applied as part of the examination and/or verification procedures within a specific section, the overall evaluation of internal control should be coordinated, for all procedures to be performed, with the "Table of Guidelines for Sample Design" (see the section entitled "Statistical Sampling"). Frequently, it is more efficient to use a single sample for several examination and/or verification procedures, use of a single sample requires the employment of the least effective control evaluation.

Specific weaknesses and related recommendations should be fully documented in the related section of the questionnaire. In addition, all weaknesses and recommendations should be summarized in the applicable spaces on the summary page of the questionnaire to facilitate review and incorporation in the report of examination. Significant recommendations should be discussed with bank management and a memorandum of the discussion should be prepared and filed in the working papers.

The questionnaire has been designed to apply to a wide range of systems and, consequently, is general. Accordingly, not all sections and/or questions will be applicable to every situation, depending on factors, such as bank size, complexity and type of operations, and organizational structure. When completing the questionnaire, the examiner should include a brief comment stating the reason a section or question is not applicable to the specific situation.

For large banking institutions or when multiple locations of a bank are being examined, it may be necessary to design supplements to the questionnaire in order to adequately review all phases of the bank's operations and related internal controls. Because certain functions described in this handbook may be performed by several departments in some banks, it also may be necessary to redesign a particular section of the questionnaire so that each department receives appropriate consideration. Conversely, functions described in several different sections of this handbook may be performed in a single department in smaller banks. For example, the lending functions described in the sections "Commercial Loans," "Accounts Receivable Financing," "Floor Plan Loans," and "Real Estate Loans" may be incorporated into a single department under the direction and control of a single loan officer. In such circumstances, the examiner should modify the questionnaire to fit the particular circumstances and to avoid duplication of questions. If the questionnaire is adapted to fit a specific situation, care should be taken to insure that its scope and intent are not modified. That requires professional judgment in interpreting and expanding the generalized material. Any such modifications should be completely documented and filed in the working papers.

Internal and External Audits
Section 102.1

INTRODUCTION

The introduction to this handbook states that the examiner's role, under ideal circumstances, is to make a qualitative analysis of the bank under examination. That may be accomplished by performing the examination procedures prescribed for each area of interest, including an evaluation of a bank's internal controls. Verification procedures, satisfactorily performed as a part of internal or external audit functions, would not be duplicated by the examiner.

This section provides guidelines to assist the examiner in understanding and evaluating the objectives of, and the work performed by, internal and external auditors. It also sets forth the general criteria that should be considered by the examiner in determining if the work of internal and external auditors is acceptable.

The Office of the Comptroller of the Currency (OCC) acknowledges the assistance it has received from the Audit Commission of Bank Administration Institute with respect to certain of the material presented herein.

INTERNAL AUDITS

Traditionally, the primary objectives of the internal audit function in the banking industry have been the detection of irregularities and the determination of compliance with a bank's policies and procedures. Internal auditors have been properly concerned with ascertaining whether the procedures and methods used for recording and processing transactions are in compliance with the policies prescribed in the internal control standards set forth by the board of directors and senior management. As part of their audit program, internal auditors perform tests and other procedures that enable them to reach these determinations and that include, in many instances, the verification procedures in this handbook.

However, the responsibilities of internal auditors have expanded to include the appraisal of the soundness and adequacy of accounting, operating, and administrative controls. Such appraisal is intended to ensure that these controls provide for the prompt and accurate recording of transactions and the proper safeguarding of assets. In addition, internal auditors often have the responsibility of participating, when appropriate, in the formation of new, and the revision of existing policies and procedures. Such participation ensures that adequate safeguards and controls, including appropriate evidential matter and audit trails, are provided during the planning and implementation process. Additional responsibilities of internal auditors may also include determining the bank's compliance with applicable laws, rules, and regulations; evaluating the effectiveness of administrative controls and procedures; and evaluating the efficiency of operations. The latter responsibility is often referred to as operational auditing.

In the absence of detailed standards promulgated by professional associations of internal auditors, such as the Bank Administration Institute (BAI) and the Institute of Internal Auditors, the OCC believes that examiners should evaluate a bank's program of internal audit based on the general criteria discussed later in this section. If detailed standards are developed for internal auditors in the future, the OCC will review them and, to the extent considered appropriate, incorporate them in the procedures to be followed by examiners.

The major factors that must be considered by the examiner in reviewing and evaluating the internal audit function are the competence and independence of the internal auditors and the adequacy and effectiveness of the audit program.

COMPETENCE OF AUDITORS

The responsibilities of internal auditors and their qualifications will vary depending on the size and complexity of a bank's operations and on the emphasis placed on the audit function by the directorate and management. In many banks, the internal audit function is performed by an individual or group that has no other responsibility. In large banks, the chief auditor is often a manager who fulfills his or her responsibilities through the work of other people. In other banks, particularly smaller ones, the responsibility for internal audit may be placed with an officer or employee designated as a part-time auditor. In yet other instances, several employees may divide the audit responsibility. Internal auditors often are responsible directly to the board of directors, or a committee thereof, rather than to management. The qualifications discussed below, therefore, should not be viewed as minimum requirements; rather, they are intended to be matters that the examiner must consider in evaluating the work performed by the specific internal auditors or audit departments.

The manager of an internal audit department should have qualifications that may not be found in all the members of the audit staff. The examiner should expect, for example, to find that the manager of internal audit:

1 Possesses a college degree with a business major or comparable business experience.
2 Is committed to a program of continuing education and professional development.

3 Has audit experience and possesses organizational and technical skills commensurate with the responsibilities assigned.

4 Demonstrates an ability to communicate with others, both orally and in writing.

To fully understand the flow of data and the underlying operating procedures, the internal audit department manager must possess the proper education and training. College courses are one source; however, adequate education may be achieved through participation in courses sponsored by industry groups, such as BAI, or through in-house training programs. Significant work experience in various departments of a bank also may provide adequate training. Certification as a Chartered Bank Auditor, Certified Internal Auditor, or Certified Public Accountant serves as evidence of meeting the educational requirements. In addition to prior education, the auditor should be committed to a program of continuing education that may include attending technical meetings and seminars and reviewing current literature on auditing and banking. The auditor's organizational skills should be reflected in the audit program and its effectiveness. Technical skills may be demonstrated through the use of techniques such as internal control and other questionnaires, testing (including statistical sampling), flowcharting, and computer programming.

In considering the qualifications of the audit staff, the examiner should review the educational and experience qualifications required by the bank for the position to be filled in the audit department and the training available for that position. In addition, the examiner must be assured that any member of the audit staff functioning as a supervisor possesses an adequate knowledge of audit objectives and an understanding of the audit procedures performed by the staff.

In a small bank, it is not uncommon to find that the

internal audit, whether full- or part-time, is a one-person department. Such an auditor may plan and perform all audits personnally, or may direct staff borrowed from other departments. In either case, the examiner should expect as a minimum that the auditor possesses qualifications similar to those of a staff supervisor as described above.

The final measure of the competence of the internal auditor is the quality of the work performed and the ability to communicate the results of that work. Accordingly, the examiner's conclusions with respect to an auditor's competence also should reflect the adequacy of the audit program and the audit reports.

INDEPENDENCE OF AUDITORS

The ability of the internal audit function to achieve its objectives depends in large part on the independence maintained by audit personnel. Frequently, an indication of the auditor's independence may be obtained by determining where he or she is located administratively within the organization and to whom, or to what level, he or she reports the results of the work performed. In ideal circumstances, the internal audit function is under the direction of the board of directors or a committee thereof. That enables the audit function to assist the directors in fulfilling their responsibilities.

An analysis of the reporting process followed by the auditor and of the findings and recommendations in the audit reports also is important in determining the auditor's duties. The auditor should be given the authority necessary to perform the job. That authority should include free access to any records necessary for the proper conduct of the audit.

Internal auditors must maintain independence in appearance as well as in fact. Accordingly, they should be instructed in the standards they are required to meet in their individual behavior and in the performance of their field work.

PROGRAM ADEQUACY

The factors that should be considered in assessing the adequacy of the audit program are:

Scope and frequency of the audit work
Documentation of the work performed
Content of the audit programs
Conclusions reached and reports issued

The scope of the program of internal audit must be sufficient to attain the audit objectives. The frequency with which the audit procedures are performed should be based on an evaluation of the risk associated with each area of audit interest. Among the factors that the auditor should consider in assessing risk are the nature of the specific operation and related assets and liabilities, the existence of appropriate policies and internal control standards, the effectiveness of operating procedures and internal controls, and the potential materiality of errors or irregularities associated with the specific operation.

For the examiner to have a sound basis upon which to evaluate the adequacy of the internal audit program, there must exist a documented record of the work performed. Such a record is best created through the completion of audit working papers. The examiner should expect such working papers to contain, among other things, audit work programs and analyses that clearly indicate the procedures performed, the extent of the testing, and the basis for the conclusions reached.

Although audit work programs are an integral part of the working papers, they are sufficiently important to deserve separate attention. Work programs serve as the primary evidence of the audit procedures performed and, as such, they should be written and should cover all areas of a bank's operations. Each program should provide a clear, concise description of the audit work required, and individual audit procedures should be presented in a logical manner. The detailed procedures included in the program will vary depending on, among other factors, the size and complexity of the bank's operations. In addition, an individual audit work program may encompass several departments of the bank, a single department, or specific operations within a department. Most audit programs, however, will include procedures similar to those contained in the OCC's verification programs:

Surprise examinations, where appropriate
Maintenance of control over records selected for audit
Review and evaluation of the bank's policies and procedures, and the system of internal control
Proof of detail to related control records
Verification of selected transactions and/or balances through procedures such as
    Examination of supporting documentation
    Direct confirmation and appropriate follow-up of exceptions
    Physical inspection

Completion of the specific procedures included in all work programs should enable the internal auditor to reach conclusions that will satisfy the related audit objectives. Also, such conclusions should be appropriate in view of the work performed. Audit reports that are prepared must be consistent with such conclusions. In addition, such reports should include, when appropriate, recommendations by the internal auditor for any required remedial actions.

PROGRAM EFFECTIVENESS

The effectiveness of any internal audit program depends upon a variety of factors. The adequacy of the audit program is, of course, one of those factors, as is proper planning. To plan properly, the auditor must consider all of the factors previously discussed in this section together with those included in "Examination Planning and Control." A third factor in determining the effectiveness of the internal audit function is the supervision and review of the audit work performed, which should be appropriate to the competence of the individuals performing the auditing, and the difficulty of the individual areas of audit interest and their degree of risk.

The examiner should also analyze the reporting process because required changes in the bank's internal controls and operating procedures can be made only if appropriate officials are informed of the deficiencies. That means that the auditor must communicate all findings and recommendations in a clear, concise manner, pinpointing problems and suggesting solutions. It also requires that the auditor submit reports as soon after the completion of the related work as practicable and that the report be routed to those officials who have both the responsibility and authority to implement suggested changes. Prompt and effective management response to the auditor's recommendations is the final measure of the effectiveness of the audit program.

AUDIT REVIEW

The examiner's review and evaluation of the internal audit functions should be included in the pre-examination analysis and review of the bank (see "Examination Planning and Control") as it is a key element in determining the scope of the examination. In most situations, the competence and independence of the internal auditors may be reviewed on an overall basis. The adequacy and effectiveness of the audit program, however, should be determined separately for each area of examination interest. In most circumstances, the examiner should use the Audit Function Questionnaire to determine if sufficient internal audit procedures are performed in each area of examination interest.

Based on the evaluation of relevant factors, the examiner should conclude whether the work performed by the internal auditors is acceptable, partially acceptable, or not acceptable. Often it is more efficient for the examiner to determine the competence and independence of the internal auditor before addressing the adequacy and effectiveness of the audit program. If, for example, the examiner concludes that the internal auditor possesses neither the competence nor the independence deemed appropriate, there is no choice but to conclude that the audit work performed is not acceptable. Accordingly, a review of such work may not be necessary.

The concept of partial reliance or acceptability applies only to the review and evaluation of the internal audit function. There may be situations in which the examiner detects certain weaknesses in the overall audit function or in the auditing procedures applicable to a specific area that are not of such magnitude as to lead to a conclusion that the audit function is not acceptable. In such situations, the examiner should conclude that the audit function is partially acceptable. For example, if the internal auditor is independent and has performed the appropriate audit procedures for commercial loans within the past year, but has little experience or training in auditing, the examiner would properly conclude that the audit function was partially acceptable.

The Audit Function Questionnaire is intentionally designed to cover the audit objectives in general terms. The questionnaire is intended to assist examiners in arriving at an overall conclusion for each area of examination interest. Accordingly, it ordinarily would not be necessary or desirable to attempt to match specific steps in the verification program with ones in the internal audit programs because in most instances, a number of different procedures could be performed to accomplish an overall audit objective. An examiner may conclude that the audit function is acceptable in a specific area but that a significant audit procedure, such as confirmation of account balances, was not performed. In such a situation, the examiner should perform those significant verification procedures not included in the internal auditor's program.

Although the OCC recognizes that the frequency of internal audit procedures should be based on an evaluation of risk associated with each area of audit interest, reliance on the work of internal auditors requires that the OCC establish general frequency guidelines applicable to most situations. Accordingly, most internal audit procedures are expected to be performed annually. It is recognized that occasionally the time between the performance of certain audit procedures will exceed 12 months. However, the OCC believes that the elapsed time should ordinarily not exceed 18 months. There may be situations in which the associated risk is considered minimal due to, among other factors, the materiality of the amounts involved, the internal control procedures followed, and the bank's history in a particular area. For example, in many large banks with extensive systems of branches, internal audits of cash on hand at the branches may be scheduled on a rotating basis once every one or two years. Such a program of rotating cash counts frequently is combined with periodic surprise counts of cash by branch officers. In that and analogous situations, the examiner may conclude that sufficient evidence exists to accept the frequency followed by the internal auditor. Such conclusions should be supported by appropriate information in the working papers.

EXTERNAL AUDITS

The by-laws of many national banks require that certain examination procedures, as determined by the board of directors, be performed periodically. Such examinations are referred to hereinafter as directors' examinations. External auditors frequently are engaged to assist the directorate in meeting this requirement and in many cases the auditors are Certified Public Accountants (CPA's). Often, however, the work is performed by other groups, such as "bank auditors," "auditors," "accountants," or occasionally, the internal audit department of a correspondent bank or bank holding company. In other instances, the directorate may consider that the program of internal audit is sufficient to satisfy the requirement. The directors should participate in the examination at least to the extent of appraising the bank's policies and the procedures used to attain their objectives and of reviewing the examination report with the auditors.

External auditors, particularly CPA's, provide services in the areas of auditing and special studies in addition to directors' examinations. Bank holding companies whose securities are subject to the Securities Exchange Act of 1934 are required to have their financial statements examined by a CPA. In other instances, directors may elect to employ external auditors to examine the year-end financial statements of the bank and to render a report based on such examination. Thus the directors are able to receive outside assurance of the validity of the bank's financial position and results of operations and can include the auditors' report in their annual report to shareholders.

External auditors and consultants also are often engaged to conduct in-depth reviews of the operations of specific departments, such as commercial loans or data processing. Such reviews might focus on operations procedures, personnel requirements or other specific areas of interest. Upon completion of such reviews, the auditors may recommend that the bank, among other things, strengthen controls and/or increase efficiency. Banks often employ external auditors as well as other specialists to assist management in specialized fields, such as taxation and management information systems.

Services provided by external auditors are performed at various times during the year. The directors' examination is performed at least once a year, with the date varying. Financial statements are examined annually and generally commence in the latter part of the year, with the report issued shortly after the start of the new year. Other types of examinations or reviews are performed at various dates on an "as required" basis.

The objective of an external audit is different from the objectives of an internal audit or a bank examination. In general, external audits are aimed at enabling the accountant to express an opinion on the financial statements. For directors' examinations, the accountant describes the procedures performed and the related findings. In either case, many of the steps included under examination and verifications procedures in this handbook are similar to the procedures performed during an audit or a directors' examination.

The examiner is interested in the work performed by external auditors for three principal reasons. First, situations will arise where internal audit work is not being performed or where such work is deemed to be of limited value (partially acceptable) or no value (unacceptable) to the examiner. In such situations, the work performed by external auditors should be reviewed to determine if it may be relied on in lieu of the examiner performing the necessary verification procedures. Second, the work performed by external auditors may affect the amount of testing the examiner must perform. Third, reports rendered by external auditors often provide the examiner with information pertinent to the examination of the bank.

The major factors that should be considered in evaluating work of external auditors are similar to those applicable to internal auditors, namely, the competence and independence of the auditors and the adequacy of the audit program.

CERTIFIED PUBLIC ACCOUNTANTS

The following paragraphs deal with the standards for competence and independence of CPA's as well as the auditing standards to be followed by them in connection with their audits of financial statements and their reports as promulgated by the American Institute of Certified Public Accountants (AICPA). All CPA's are not members of the AICPA; however, all must follow professional standards adopted whether by their respective state societies or the state agency issuing their licenses.

In the performance of their work, CPA's must be independent of those they serve. Traditionally, independence has been defined as the ability to act with integrity and objectivity. The Code of Professional Ethics as adopted by the AICPA states, in part:

> When a CPA expresses an opinion on financial statements not only the fact but also the appearance of integrity and objectivity is of particular importance. For this reason, the profession has adopted rules to prohibit the expression of such an opinion when relationships exist which might pose such a threat to integrity and objectivity as to exceed the strength of countervailing forces and restraints. These relationships fall into two general categories: (a) certain financial relationships with clients, and (b) relationships in which the CPA is virtually part of management or an employee under management control.

In accordance with the rule on independence included in the Code of Professional Ethics and related AICPA interpretations, the independence of a CPA will be considered to be impaired if, during the period of his or her professional engagement, the CPA or his or her firm had any direct or material indirect financial interest in the enterprise or had a loan to or from the enterprise or any officer, director, or principal stockholder thereof. This latter proscription does not apply to the following loans from a financial institution when made under normal lending procedures, terms and requirements: (1) loans obtained by a CPA or his or her firm which are not material in relation to the net worth of such borrower, (2) home mortgages, and (3) other secured loans, except loans guaranteed by a CPA's firm which are otherwise unsecured.

Additionally, the OCC and the Securities and Exchange Commission require that all CPA firms that practice before them be independent. 12 CFR 11.7 and SEC rule 2-01 of Regulation S-X state, in part:

> The OCC (Commission) will not recognize any certified public accountant as independent who is not in fact independent . . .

> In determining whether an accountant may in fact be not independent with respect to a particular person, the OCC (Commission) will give appropriate consideration to all relevant circumstances, including evidence bearing on all relationships between the accountant and that person or any affiliate thereof, and will not confine itself to the relationships existing in connection with the filing of reports with the OCC (Commission).

CPA's also are required by their Code of Professional Ethics to perform their examinations, referred to herinafter as audits, within the framework of generally accepted auditing standards. Auditing standards, as distinct from auditing procedures, are concerned not only with the auditor's professional qualifications, but also with the judgment exercised in the performance of an audit and with the resulting reports. Generally accepted auditing standards are grouped into three categories: general standards, standards of field work, and standards of reporting.

The general standards require that the examination be

performed by a person or persons having adequate technical training and proficiency, that an independence in mental attitude be maintained, and that due professional care be exercised in the performance of the audit and the preparation of the report.

CPA's possess basic education in accounting and auditing or equivalent experience which is required as a prerequisite for taking the uniform CPA examination. Several states have made continuing education a requirement for renewing a CPA license. Field work standards include requirements that:

1   The work be adequately planned.
2   Assistants, if any, be properly supervised.
3   A proper study and evaluation of existing internal controls be made as a basis for reliance thereon for the determination of audit scope and audit procedures, including the extent of testing.
4   Sufficient evidence be obtained to afford a reasonable basis for an opinion regarding the financial statements under audit.

The reporting standards deserve particular attention, because examiners must understand CPA's. Reporting standards require that the CPA state whether the financial statements are presented in accordance with generally accepted accounting principles and whether such principles have been consistently applied in the current period in relation to the preceding period. In addition, the informative disclosures in the financial statements must be reasonably adequate or the CPA must state otherwise in the report.

The report must contain an expression of opinion regarding the financial statements taken as a whole, or an assertion to the effect that an opinion cannot be expressed. Any reasons for the CPA's being unable to express an overall opinion on the financial statements also must be stated in the report.

Although the reports issued by CPA's at the conclusion of their examinations of financial statements vary, for the purposes of this discussion they have been limited to two general types. The first, commonly referred to as the short-form report, generally consists of two paragraphs; the first or scope paragraph identifies the financial statements examined and describes generally the work performed, and the second paragraph contains an expression of the CPA's opinion. Generally, the following form is used for short-form unqualified opinions:

> We have examined the balance sheet of the First National Bank of Anytown as of December 31, 19XX, and the related statements of income, retained earnings, and changes in financial position for the year then ended. Our examination was made in accordance with generally accepted auditing standards and, accordingly, included such tests of the accounting records and such other auditing procedures as we considered necessary in the circumstances.

> In our opinion, the financial statements referred to above present fairly the financial position of the First National Bank of Anytown as of December 31, 19XX, and the results of its operations and the changes in its financial position for the year then ended, in conformity with generally accepted accounting principles applied on a basis consistent with that of the preceding year.

Any modifying language, either in the description of the scope of the auditor's work or in the opinion, should be considered as qualifying the opinion in some manner, except when the auditor's opinion is based in part on the report of another auditor. Departure from the auditor's standard report may be required by the following circumstances:

1 The scope of the audit has been restricted by the bank or has been affected by conditions that do not permit the application of auditing procedures considered necessary in the circumstances.

2 Inadequate disclosure or lack of conformity with generally accepted accounting principles affect the financial statements in that they do not fairly present financial conditions, results of operations, or changes in financial position.

3 Accounting principles have not been applied consistently.

4 Unusual uncertainties exist as to the outcome of future events, and their effect on the financial statements cannot be reasonably estimated.

When the exception is material, but not so material as to negate an opinion on the financial statements taken as a whole, a qualified opinion is appropriate. What is sufficiently material is a matter of judgment in the circumstances. If the matter is related to the scope of the procedures or the fairness of presentation of the financial statements, the phrase "except for" is normally used. The phrase "subject to" is used properly only in situations where an uncertainty exists.

An adverse opinion is issued by the auditor when the matter taken exception to is so pervasive in effect that the financial statements do not present fairly the financial position, results of operations, or change in financial position, and/or are not in conformity with generally accepted accounting principles.

A disclaimer of opinion is issued when the scope of the auditor's examination has been restricted in important respects, either by the bank or by circumstances, or when the financial statements are affected by uncertainties.

In the case of a qualified, adverse or disclaimer of opinion, the auditor should set forth all material reasons for issuing the particular report form. As to limitations of scope, the report would specify any generally accepted auditing procedures which were omitted and the reasons for omission. If the omission had been requested by the bank, that should be specified.

The second general type of report that the examiner should recognize is the long-form report. In its use in the banking industry, this type of report generally includes a more detailed description of the scope of the CPA's examination than is found in the short-form report. The AICPA has indicated that the comments on audit scope included in the long-form report should:

> . . . set forth generally the extent of the auditor's review and tests including the inspection; observation; inquiry and confirmation work relating to the various asset and liability accounts, income and expense accounts, memorandum accounts, and other phases of the audit not directly related to the accounting records. The comments should also include any exceptions noted during the audit.*

Suggestions for improving the bank's internal controls, accounting procedures and other matters may be included in the long-form report or may be the subject of a separate letter report. Although the long-form report provides this additional information, the departures from the CPA's standard report that are described in the preceding paragraphs are applicable to long-form reports.

The AICPA also has published a banking industry audit guide, which was prepared by its Committee of Bank Accounting and Auditing. The guide was published to advise AICPA members in auditing and reporting on financial statements of banks. Factors to be considered in performing a bank audit are contained in the guide to serve as the foundation of the auditing work performed by CPAs.

ENGAGEMENT LETTERS

It is not uncommon for a bank to require that external auditors submit engagement letters to the bank or its director-

*American Institute of Certified Public Accountants, Audits of Banks including Supplement, 1969.

ate prior to commencing their work. Such letters include, among other things, the scope of the audit, the period of time to be covered by the audit, and the reports expected to be rendered. In many cases, the highlights of these matters will be summarized in the body of the letter, with greater detail being provided in schedules or appendices. Procedures may be specific by audit area. That is, the auditor may provide a capsulized description of procedures with regard to cash and due from banks, loans, deposits, etc. In addition, if there are any limitations on the scope of the audit, the letter may specify any auditing procedures to be omitted, such as confirmation of loans or deposits if the auditor is expected to render an opinion on the bank's financial statements.

AUDIT REVIEW

The examination procedures program for this section contain the detailed steps to be followed by the examiner in conducting a review of CPA's and the work they perform. The following paragraphs discuss certain of the criteria the OCC considered in developing those procedures.

The OCC has concluded, that in view of its objectives regarding the reliance to be placed on work performed by CPA's and in view of the professional and ethical standards of the public accounting professions, that only in unusual situations should the examiner conduct an in-depth review of the competence and independence of the CPA or of the adequacy of the CPA's audit. One situation that the examiner should investigate would be a recent change in CPA's by a bank, particularly if the change were made after an audit was commenced.

It ordinarily will not be necessary to make specific tests to determine independence. However, there may be occasions when the examiner may have sufficient reason to question the independence of a CPA or the quality of his or her work. For example, the examiner may become aware that, during the period of a CPA's professional engagement, which includes the period covered by the financial statements on which the CPA has expressed an opinion, the CPA or a member of his or her firm:

Had a direct financial interest in the bank.

Was connected with the bank in a capacity equivalent to that of a member of management or was a director of the bank.

Maintained, completely or in part, the books and records of the bank and did not perform audit tests with respect to such books and records; or,

Had an unsecured loan from the bank that was considered to be material relative to the net worth of the borrower.

In such instances, and that list is by no means all inclusive, the CPA would not have complied with professional standards. Accordingly, the examiner should not rely on any work performed by the CPA without a review of the procedures followed in performing the audit. Such a review may require the examiner to request, through the bank, that the CPA make available appropriate working papers. The CPA's working papers should be reviewed in light of the applicable criteria discussed under "Internal Audits" and the minimum procedures outlined in the Audit Function Questionnaire. If the procedures satisfy the examiner's requirements, he or she may rely on the work performed. The examiner may conclude, however, that the circumstances, and their attendant risks, preclude the acceptance of the work performed by the CPA. In such cases, no reliance should be placed on the CPA's examination. The OCC believes that such situations will be rare, and therefore they should be discussed with the regional administrator prior to requesting the CPA's working papers or concluding that the CPA's examination is not acceptable. The circumstances, procedures followed, findings, and conclusions should be clearly described in the examiner's working papers.

The examiner should determine the scope of the CPA's

examination by reviewing the last report issued by the CPA and, if the audit is in progress or is planned to commence in the near future, any engagement letter to the bank from the CPA should be reviewed. The examiner also should obtain and review any adjusting journal entries suggested by the CPA at the conclusion of his or her examination to determine if such entries are normal recurring accruals or if the entries indicate inadequate accounting records. There will be situations where the examiner finds that the CPA was instructed to omit certain procedures that are required by generally accepted auditing standards and that are included in the examiner's verification procedures. In that situation, the examiner should place no reliance on the CPA's examination for the procedures omitted.

Under certain circumstances, a CPA may issue a qualified or adverse opinion or may disclaim an opinion on a bank's financial statements. In such circumstances, the examiner should first determine the reasons for the particular type of opinion issued. If the matters involved affect specific areas of the bank's operations which are covered by one or several verification programs, the examiner may be in a position to rely on the procedures by the CPA in all other areas of interest. If the examiner is not able to relate the matters involved to specific verification programs or procedures, no reliance should be placed on the procedures performed by the CPA.

EXTERNAL AUDITS BY OTHERS

There will be situations in which the external auditing is performed by individuals who are not certified public accountants. Examples of others who may perform such an audit include the internal auditing group of a related organization, e.g. a bank holding company, or the internal auditing department of a correspondent bank. Both of these groups are "external" insofar as the audited bank is concerned. Such auditing may afford the examiner the same reliability as auditing performed by CPA's. The principal differences, as far as the examiner is concerned, are the absence of professional standards of competence and independence and the lack of circumstances requiring the auditor to maintain the confidence of the public, as well as various regulatory authorities, in his or her role as an independent agent. Accordingly, the general criteria contained in the program External Audits – Non-CPA's is very similar to the criteria for reviewing and evaluating internal audits.

MULTI-BANK HOLDING COMPANIES

The following guidelines have been established to assist the examiner in assessing the work performed by external auditors in situations in which that work relates only to the consolidated financial statements of multi-bank holding companies:

If the bank represents more than 50 percent of the consolidated assets of the bank holding company after elimination of intercompany accounts, the examiner should assume that the CPA has performed sufficient testing of the bank's balance sheet, or

If the bank represents more than 50 percent of the consolidated net income of the bank holding company after elimination of intercompany accounts, the examiner should assume the CPA has performed sufficient testing of the bank's income statement.

If neither of the other statements apply, and the examiner is furnished with information from a CPA which indicates that the audit procedures that were performed resulted in tests at least as extensive as those that would be performed under the OCC's statistical sampling plan, the examiner may consider the CPA's audit procedures to be sufficiently extensive.

The examiner may believe that specific circumstances exist that would alter the result obtained by following the guidelines discussed above. Accordingly, such circumstances should be discussed with the regional administrator at the conclusion of the pre-examination analysis.

INTERNAL AND EXTERNAL AUDITS EXAMINATION OBJECTIVES
Section 102.2

1 To determine whether internal and external audit functions exist.
2 To evaluate the independence of those who provide the internal and external audit functions.
3 To evaluate the competence of those who provide the internal and external audit functions.
4 To determine the procedures performed by the internal and external auditors.
5 To determine, based upon the above criteria, the reliance that can be placed on the procedures performed by internal and external auditors.

INTERNAL AND EXTERNAL AUDITS AUDIT FUNCTION QUESTIONNAIRE
Section 102.4

Review reports and the appropriate programs and working papers of the auditors in order to answer the following audit function questions. Where appropriate, supporting documentation and pertinent information should be retained or noted under comments.

For the following areas, has the internal or external auditor within the last 18 months:

CASH ACCOUNTS

1 Verified cash on hand (verification should have included confirmation of incoming or outgoing cash shipments)?
2 Reviewed cash items for propriety of amount and classification?
3 Verified clearings (verification must have included confirmation procedures) and reviewed all incoming returned items for some period subsequent to the date clearings were verified?
4 Checked adherence to procedures for maintaining records in accordance with 31 CFR 103.22, 103.23, 103.33 and 103.34?
5 Checked deposit, cash and, withdrawal tickets or comparable documents for possible violations of 31 CFR 103?
6 Reviewed cash control records and traced any apparently large or unusual cash movements to or from a department or branch?

DUE FROM BANKS

1 Tested bank reconcilements including the Federal Reserve bank?
2 Received cut-off bank statements as of the examination date and an appropriate date subsequent to the examination date for use in testing bank reconcilements?
3 Reviewed all returned items for an appropriate period subsequent to the examination date?

4 Confirmed due from banks—time accounts with the banks holding the deposits?

INVESTMENTS

1 Verified investment securities balances (verification must have included physical count of securities located at the bank and confirmation of securities held outside the bank or in transit)?

2 Checked the book and market value of investment securities?

3 Checked the gain and loss of investment securities sold during the period?

4 Reviewed the accrued interest accounts and checked computation of interest income?

BANK DEALER ACTIVITIES

1 Verified securities balances (verification must have included physical count of securities located at the bank and confirmation of securities held outside the bank or in transit)?

2 Checked the book and market value of trading account securities?

3 Checked the gain and loss on underwriting and trading account transactions?

4 Reviewed the accrued interest accounts and checked computation of interest income?

5 Verified "fails" and "due bills" (verification must have included confirmation procedures)?

6 Verified good faith deposits and cash collateral (verification must have included confirmation procedures)?

LOANS

Commercial

1 Verified loan balances (verification must have included confirmation procedures)?
2 Examined, or confirmed with outside custodian, notes and other legal documentation, including collateral?
3 Tested the pricing of negotiable collateral?
4 Determined that any necessary insurance coverage is adequate and the bank is named as loss payee?
5 Reviewed the accrued interest accounts and tested computation of interest income?

Accounts Receivable Financing

1 Verified loan balances (verification must have included confirmation procedures)?
2 Examined, or confirmed with outside custodian, notes and other legal documentation, including collateral?
3 Determined that any necessary insurance coverage is adequate and the bank is named as loss payee?
4 Reviewed the accrued interest accounts and checked computation of interest income?

Direct Lease Financing

1 Verified leases and related balance sheet accounts (verification must have included confirmation procedures)?
2 Examined leases and other legal documentation?
3 Checked computation of depreciation expense?
4 Checked computation of interest and/or rent income?
5 Checked computation of gain or loss on property sales

and disposals and traced sales proceeds to cash receipts
records?

6 Determined that any deferred tax liability or asset is
accurately reflected?

7 Checked computation of investment tax credit?

8 Reviewed insurance coverage and determined that property
coverage is adequate in relation to book value and
that liability insurance is in effect?

Installment

1 Verified loan balances (verification must have included
confirmation procedures)?

2 Examined, or confirmed with outside custodian, notes
and other legal documentation including collateral?

3 Determined that any necessary insurance coverage is
adequate and the bank is named as loss payee?

4 Verified unearned discount and any accrued interest balances
and checked the computation of interest income?

5 Reviewed sales of repossessed collateral and determined
the propriety of the entries made to record the sales?

6 Tested rebate amounts for loans which have been prepaid?

Floor Plan

1 Verified loan balances (verification must have included
confirmation procedures)?

2 Examined, or confirmed with outside custodian, notes
and other legal documentation?

3 Physically inspected collateral?

4 Determined that any necessary insurance coverage is
adequate and the bank is named as loss payee?

5   Reviewed the accrued interest accounts and checked the computation of interest income?

Credit Card

1   Verified loan balances (verification must have included confirmation procedures)?
2   Checked the computation of interest income?

Check Credit

1   Verified loan balances (verification must have included confirmation procedures)?
2   Examined, or confirmed with outside custodian, notes and other legal documentation?
3   Checked computation of interest (and service fee, if applicable) income?

Real Estate

1   Verified loan and escrow account balances (verification must have included confirmation procedures)?
2   Examined, or confirmed with outside custodian, notes and other legal documentation, including collateral?
3   Determined that any necessary insurance coverage is adequate and the bank is named as loss payee?
4   Reviewed the accrued interest accounts and checked computation of interest income?

Construction

1   Verified loan balances (verification must have included confirmation procedures)?
2   Examined, or confirmed with outside custodian, notes and legal documentation, including collateral?

3   Verified contingency or escrow account balances?
4   Reviewed the accrued interest accounts and checked computation of interest income?

RESERVE FOR POSSIBLE LOAN LOSSES

1   Verified loan balances for loans charged off since their last examination (verification must have included confirmation procedures) and amounts of debit entries to the reserve account?
2   Examined supporting documentation for loans charged off?
3   Reviewed loan recoveries and agreed amounts to credit entries in the reserve account?
4   Tested transfers from (to) undivided profits and the recording of deferred tax credits (charges) if the deduction for loan losses on the bank's tax return was different from that charged to operations?

BANK PREMISES AND EQUIPMENT

1   Examined support for additions, sales, and disposals?
2   Reviewed property transactions with "bank affiliated personnel"?
3   Verified property balances?
4   Checked computation of depreciation expense?
5   Checked computation of gain or loss on property sales and disposals and traced sales proceeds to cash receipt records?
6   Determined that any deferred tax liability or asset, that may evolve from the use of different depreciation

methods for book and tax purposes, is accurately reflected?

7 Checked computation of investment tax credit?

OTHER ASSETS

1 Verified other asset balances?

2 Examined support for additions and disposals?

3 Reviewed the computation of any gains or losses on disposals?

4 Reviewed the bank's computation of any amortization?

5 Reviewed inter-office transactions?

6 Reviewed suspense accounts to determine whether all items included were temporary?

DEPOSITS

Demand and Other Transaction Accounts

1 Verified account balances (verification must have included confirmation procedures)?

2 Reviewed closed accounts and determined that they were properly closed?

3 Reviewed account activity in dormant accounts, bank-controlled accounts (such as dealers' reserves), employee/officer accounts, and accounts of employees'/officers' business interests?

4 Reviewed overdraft accounts and determined collection potential?

5 Checked computation of service charges and traced postings to appropriate income accounts?

Time

1 Verified time deposit account balances (verification must have included confirmation procedures)?
2 Reviewed closed accounts and determined that they were properly closed?
3 Reviewed activity in dormant accounts, bank-controlled accounts, employee/officer accounts, and accounts of employees'/officers' business interests?
4 Reviewed the accrued interest accounts and checked computations of interest expense?
5 Accounted for numerical sequence of prenumbered certificates of deposit?

Official Checks

1 Reconciled account balances?
2 Determined the validity and completeness of outstanding checks?
3 Examined documentation supporting paid checks?
4 Tested certified checks to customer's collected funds balances?

BORROWED FUNDS

1 Verified borrowed funds balances (verification must have included confirmation procedures)?
2 Examined supporting legal documents and determined compliance therewith?
3 Reviewed minutes of the stockholders' and board of directors' meetings for approval of all borrowing requiring such approval?

4 Verified changes in capital notes outstanding?

5 Reviewed the accrued interest accounts and checked computation of interest expense?

OTHER LIABILITIES

1 Verified balances of "other liability" accounts (verification procedures must include tests for unrecorded liabilities as of a given date)?

2 Reviewed the operation and use of the "interoffice" account?

3 Reviewed suspense accounts to determine whether all items cleared on a timely basis?

CAPITAL ACCOUNTS AND DIVIDENDS

Capital Stock

1 If a bank acts as its own transfer agent and/or registrar, accounted for all stock certificates (issued and unissued) and reconciled par value of outstanding shares to appropriate general ledger control accounts?

2 If bank has an outside transfer agent and/or registrar, confirmed shares issued and activity since previous examination?

3 Reviewed capital changes since previous examination?

Dividends

1 Checked the computation of dividends paid and/or accrued?

2 Reviewed minutes of the board of directors' meetings to determine propriety of dividend payments and accruals?

CONSIGNED ITEMS AND OTHER NONLEDGER CONTROL ACCOUNTS

Safe Deposit Boxes

1 Tested rental income?
2 Checked vault entry records for signature(s) of authorized persons?
3 Tested reconcilements of control records?

Safekeeping/Custodial Accounts

1 Examined or confirmed with outside custodian safekeeping custodial items?
2 Tested completeness of safekeeping/custodial items and records by examining supporting documentation or by confirming with customers?
3 Tested closed safekeeping/custodial accounts?
4 Tested safekeeping/custodial fee income?

Collection Items

1 Tested collection items by examining supporting documentation, subsequent receipt of payments, disbursement to customers of funds collected, or by confirming with customers?
2 Tested collection fee income?

Consigned Items

1 Reconciled physical count of unissued and voided items on hand to memorandum controls?
2 Confirmed with consignor the inventory on hand at the bank?
3 Tested income from sale of consigned items?

INCOME AND EXPENSES

1 Tested income and expenses by examining supporting documentation for authenticity and proper approval?
2 Tested accruals by either recomputing amounts or examining documents supporting such accruals?

RELATED ORGANIZATIONS

1 Reviewed and tested the investment in and the transactions with related organizations?
2 Determined that investments, advances, or transactions with affiliates are consistent with covenants of debt or other instruments as approved by the board of directors or bank management?

"OUTSIDE" SERVICE CENTERS

1 Performed periodic audit procedures for significant automated applications to determine that work flow is processed accurately and in conformity with operating manuals?
2 Controlled or periodically reviewed dormant accounts?
3 Reviewed unposted items?

BRANCHES

Has the internal or external auditor performed appropriate audit procedures in the branches during the last 18 months which are at least as comprehensive as those listed in the applicable areas above?

DUTIES AND RESPONSIBILITIES OF DIRECTORS
Section 501.1

INTRODUCTION

Directors are placed in positions of trust by the bank's shareholders and both statute and common law place responsibility for the management of a bank firmly and squarely on the board of directors. The directors of a national bank may delegate the day-to-day routine of conducting the bank's business to their officers and employees but they cannot delegate their responsibility for the consequences of unsound or imprudent policies and practices whether it involves lending, investing, protecting against internal fraud or any other banking activity. The directorate is responsible to its depositors and shareholders for safeguarding their interests through the lawful, informed, efficient, and able administration of the institution.

The affairs of each national banking association are to be managed by directors, who initially, are elected by the shareholders at a meeting held before the association is finally authorized to commence business, and afterward at meetings to be held at least annually on a day specified in the bylaws. The directors hold office for 1 year and until their successors are elected and have qualified. The number of directors of each national association is limited to not less than five nor more than 25. Various laws govern the election, required number, qualifications, oath, liability, and removal of directors or officers, as well as disclosure requirements for outside business interests. Other laws pertain to certain restrictions, prohibitions, and penalties relating to securities dealers as directors, officers or employees, interlocking directorates, purchases from directors and sales to directors, commissions and gifts for procuring loans, embezzlement, abstraction, willful misapplications, false entries, and penalty for political contributions, and other matters. The examiner must be familiar with these laws, and the related regulations interpretive rulings, and the contents of a pamphlet issued by the Office of the Comptroller of the Currency (OCC), entitled "Duties and Liabilities of Directors of National Banks."

A record of supervisory actions by directors is to be kept, as specified by the bylaws, in a directors' meeting minute book.

DIRECTORS' RESPONSIBILITIES

An examiner sometimes has to impress bank directors with the extent of their duties and responsibilities. Unless bank directors realize the importance of their positions and act accordingly, they are failing to discharge their obligations to the shareholders and depositors. They are also failing to take advantage of the opportunity to exercise a sound and beneficial influence on the economy of their community. The following are the major responsibilities of bank directors:

1 To select competent executive officers—It is a primary duty of a board of directors to select and appoint executive officers who are qualified to administer the bank's affairs effectively and soundly. It is also the responsibility of the board to dispense with services of officers who prove unable to meet reasonable standards of executive ability and efficiency.

2 To effectively supervise the bank's affairs—The character and degree of supervision required of a bank's board of directors to assure a soundly managed bank involves

reasonable business judgment and competence, and sufficient time to become informed about the bank's affairs. Directors cannot avoid responsibility for their bank's sound management or its problems. If supervisory negligence is involved, a director's responsibility may extend to personal financial responsibility. The responsibility of directors to supervise the bank's affairs may not be delegated to the active executive officers. Directors may delegate certain authority to executive officers, but not the primary responsibility to maintain the bank and its policies on a sound and legal basis.

3   To adopt and follow sound policies and objectives—The directors must provide a clear framework of objectives and policies within which the chief executive officer must operate and administer the bank's affairs. Such objectives and policies should cover all areas. Some of the more important areas would be investments, loans, asset and liability management, profit planning and budgeting, capital planning, and personnel policies. The examination of such policies is covered in other sections of this handbook.

4   To avoid self-serving practices—A self-serving board, whether weak or strong in other respects, is a dangerous board. The fact that individuals are bank directors does not increase their borrowing privileges, it simply increases their borrowing responsibilities. A bank's directors bear a greater than normal responsibility in dealing with the loans to members of the directorate. They must make decisions that preclude the possibility of partiality or favored treatment. Unwarranted loans to a bank's directors or to their interests are a serious matter from the standpoint of credit and management. Losses that develop from such unwarranted loans are bad enough, but the weakening effect on the bank's general credit standards is likely to be even worse. Directors who become financially dependent on their bank normally lose their

usefulness as directors. Other self-serving practices to which the examiner should be alert are:

a Gratuities to directors for the purpose of obtaining their approval of financing arrangements or the use of particular services.

b The use of bank monies by directors, officers, or shareholders to obtain loans or transact other business. Directors should be especially critical of correspondent bank balances when officers, directors, or shareholders are borrowing from the depository bank. The Department of Justice is of the opinion that certain interbank deposits connected with a loan to officers, directors, or shareholders of the depositing bank might constitute a misapplication of funds in violation of 18 USC 656.

c Transactions involving conflicts of interest. These always represent potentially self-serving transactions. When board decisions involving a potential conflict of interest are made, the director should fully disclose the manner in which the transaction tends to be beneficial and should abstain from voting on the matter. The abstention should be recorded in the minutes.

5 To be informed of the bank's condition and management policies—As part of a director's responsibility to be informed of the bank's condition and management policies, the OCC requires that all national banks, under a provision in their bylaws, provide for a directors' examination. The pamphlet "Duties and Liabilities of Directors of National Banks" should serve as a guide to directors in performing their examination. That examination, conducted by the directors' examining committee, should be at least as thorough as that outlined under paragraphs 39 and 40 of the pamphlet.

When the directors lack adequate knowledge of examination techniques and procedures, they are encouraged to employ outside auditors to make some or all of the examination on their behalf. Such an examination, performed by an outside firm, is much more beneficial to the directors if the examining committee or the entire board plays an active role in it. Directors should participate at least to the extent of appraising policies, obtaining an understanding of the procedures to be employed by the auditor and reviewing the audit report with the auditors. Before concluding the review, directors should understand thoroughly the significance of all the details contained in the report. When outside auditing firms are utilized, the scope of the examination should include direct confirmation of a representative number of the bank's loans and deposits.

Copies of the directors' examination report and the reports by outside auditors should be retained in the bank's files and be made available to examiners. When an accounting firm supplements its audit report with a letter report containing recommendations for improvements in internal controls, accounting or other matters, the examiner should obtain a copy of it and should review its contents. Any significant deficiencies noted in the letter should be discussed with management to obtain correction.

6 To maintain reasonable capitalization—A board of directors has the responsibility of maintaining its bank on a well-capitalized basis. A discussion of capital planning and capital adequacy is included in "Capital Accounts" and the examiner should be familiar with the information contained therein.

7 To observe banking laws, rulings and regulations— Directors must exercise care to see that banking laws are

not violated. That duty may involve financial responsibility for losses arising out of illegal actions.

8 To ensure that the bank has a beneficial influence on the economy of its community—One reason for approving bank charters is to meet a specific community need. Directors, therefore, have a continuing responsibility to the community to provide those banking services which will be conducive to well-balanced economic growth. Directors should be certain that they attempt to satisfy all legitimate credit needs of the community. This is especially true for legitimate new and developing business credit. The examiner also should be familiar with the sections of this handbook dealing with future prospects and service area analysis.

COMPLIANCE WITH FORMAL AND INFORMAL ADMINISTRATIVE ACTIONS

Bank directors must ensure that management corrects deficiencies found in the bank. Instructions to do so may come from OCC in the form of a formal or informal administrative action, depending on the severity of the problem.

Authority for a formal action is granted by the Financial Institutions Supervisory Act of 1966 (12 USC 1818). Formal actions, or cease and disist orders and agreements, are normally exercised when banks have serious problems. For less serious problems, OCC issues a "Memorandum of Understanding." The memorandum, an informal administrative action, is an agreement between the regional administrator and the bank setting forth required corrective action.

Regional administrators are responsible for monitoring compliance with both types of administrative action. To assist in that process, the regional administrator normally receives and evaluates periodic progress reports from the bank. In addition, information is provided by the examiner, who checks compliance with the action from the date of the prior examination. The regional administrator may initiate additional supervisory action when compliance is insufficient or may recommend modifying or terminating the document upon satisfactory compliance.

The evaluation by the examiner will be discussed in the confidential portion of the report. The following format should be used:

Evaluation of Compliance with Formal or Informal Administrative Actions

1 Name of bank.
2 Nature of administrative action.
3 Date of administrative action.
4 Compliance with each article of the action.
5 Nature and extent of noncompliance, including which articles were involved.
6 Action taken to ensure compliance where noncompliance exists.
7 Significant matters requiring attention that are not currently covered by the action.
8 The effectiveness of the action, including whether additional administrative action should be taken or the outstanding action should be terminated or modified.

A copy of the completed comments together with appropriate remarks and recommendations from the regional administrator should be sent to the special projects division.

The initial decision to terminate or modify a formal administrative action rests with the regional administrator. When the regional administrator determines that such restraints have satisfactorily served their purpose, and should be removed or modified, he or she will send a memorandum to that effect accompanied by comments appearing on the evaluation form to the first deputy comptroller for operations via the special projects division. That division and the enforcement division will evaluate the recommendation together and make a joint recommendation to the Comptroller through the first deputy comptroller for operations. At the direction of the Comptroller, the enforcement and compliance division will prepare the documents necessary to terminate or modify the existing administrative action.

DEPOSITORY INSTITUTION MANAGEMENT INTERLOCKS ACT

Under Title II of the Financial Institutions Regulatory and Interest Rate Control Act of 1978, interlocking relationships of management officials of various nonaffiliated depository institutions are prohibited depending upon the asset size and geographical proximity of the organizations.

The intent of the act is to foster competition among various depository institutions by prohibiting interlocking management official relationships. However, four exceptions are permitted based on the public benefit that is derived from the interlocking relationship, and on the competitive nature of the institutions involved. The four exceptions are (1) institutions located in low-income areas or that are controlled or managed by members of a minority group or by women, (2) newly chartered institutions, (3) institutions in deteriorating condition, (4) institutions sponsoring a credit union.

Those exceptions are permissable only with prior OCC approval.

Interlocking relationships existing prior to November 10, 1978, and not in violation of 15 USC 19 are permitted to continue for a period of 10 years. Enforcement of the interlocks provisions of the act carry full cease and desist powers.

DUTIES AND RESPONSIBILITIES OF DIRECTORS
Section 501.2

EXAMINATION OBJECTIVES

1 To determine whether the board of directors fully understands its duties and responsibilities.
2 To determine if the board of directors is discharging its responsibilities in an appropriate manner.
3 To determine whether the board of directors has developed adequate objectives and policies.
4 To determine the existence of any conflicts of interest or self-dealing.
5 To determine compliance with laws, rulings and regulations.

Bibliography

Bank Administration Institute. "A Statement of Principles on Internal Auditing and The Auditor"; "Standards for Evaluating Internal Audit and Control Procedures." Board of Directors and Endorsed By The Administrative Committee of the American Bankers Association and By the Board of Directors of The Association of Reserve Bankers. Park Ridge, Ill., 1967.

Bank Administration Institute. *A Study of Internal Frauds in Banks.* Park Ridge, Ill., 1972.

Bank Administration Institute. *Auditing Bank EDP Systems.* Park Ridge, Ill., 1968.

Bank Administration Institute. *Internal Auditing in the Banking Industry,* Vols. I–III. Park Ridge, Ill., 1979.

Bank Administration Institute. *Loan Review: A Guide.* Park Ridge, Ill., 1978.

Burch, John G., Jr., and Sardinas, Joseph L., Jr. *Computer Control and Audit—A Total Systems Approach.* John Wiley and Sons, New York, 1978.

Comptroller of the Currency. *Comptroller's Handbook for National Bank Examiners–Commercial and International.* Washington, D.C., 1981.

Comptroller of the Currency. *Comptroller's Handbook for National Banks–Laws, Regulations, Interpretive Rulings.* Washington, D.C., 1981.

Comptroller of the Currency. *Comptroller's Handbook for National Trust Examiners,* Washington, D.C., 1981.

Corns, Marshall C. *How to Audit a Bank.* Bankers Publishing Co., Boston, 1966.

Davis, Gordon B. *Auditing and EDP.* American Institute of Certified Public Accountants, New York, 1968.

Hoar, Thomas A. "Computers and Audit Programs." *The Magazine of Bank Administration,* September 1979.

Hudson, Elwood F. "The Changing Role of the Auditor and Internal Controls." *The Magazine of Bank Administration,* December 1979.

Kennedy, Joseph C., and Landau, Robert. *Corporate Trust Administration and Management,* 2nd ed. New York University Press, New York, 1975.

McCormick, Peter H. "What a Bank President Expects of Audit and Control." *The Magazine of Bank Administration,* July 1980.

Nadler, Paul S. "A Bank Director's Role—Basic Questions." *Bankers Monthly,* June 1975.

Nadler, Paul S. "The Director Views The Balance Sheet." *Bankers Monthly,* September 1975.

Porter, Thomas W., and Perry, William E. *EDP Controls and Auditing,* 2nd ed. Wadsworth Publishing Company, Belmont, Calif., 1977.

Pratt, Lester A. *Bank Frauds—Their Detection and Prevention,* 2nd ed. Ronald Press, New York, 1965.

Savage, John H. *Bank Audits and Examinations.* Bankers Publishing Company, Boston, 1973.

Scott, Austin Wakeman. *Scott on Trusts.* Little, Brown and Company, Boston, 1981.

Willingham, J.J., and Carmichael, D.R. *Auditing Concepts and Methods.* McGraw-Hill Book Company, New York, 1971.

The Institute of Internal Auditors. "Statement of the Responsibilities of The Internal Auditor." New York, 1957.

Index

Operations, definition, 44, 45
Outside auditors, 16, 17
  objectives, 139

Payable through drafts, 49
Paying agent, 69
Pension trusts, nature of service,
  65
Personal trusts, nature of service,
  57
Profit sharing trusts, nature of
  service, 65
Prudent man rule, definition,
  58

Registrar, 68, 69
Resources management, 79,
  80
Risk, sources of, 133, 134,
  135
Rotation of employees, 39,
  40

Safe deposit services, 76
Savings accounts, 50, 51
Savings incentive plans, 66
Securities Exchange Acts of
  1933 and 1934, 67
Securities processing services,
  71, 72, 73
Security and protection:
  cash, 169
  data center, 162, 163, 172
  personnel, 175
  premises, 174
  requirements, 167
  safe deposit vaults, 173

securities, 170, 171
Segregation of duties, 36, 37,
  38
Special checking accounts, 49,
  50
Spot audits, 97
State bank examiners, 16, 17
Statistical sampling, 97, 98
Systems, automated, participation in design and development by auditor, 154, 155,
  156
Systems analysis and evaluation,
  control, accounting, and
  operations, 92, 93, 94, 95,
  96
Systems documentation, 156,
  157, 158

Transfer agent, 70
Trust Indenture Act of 1939,
  67
Trusts:
  corporate, 67
  employee benefit, 63
  pension, 65
  personal, 57
  profit-sharing, 65

Vacations, mandatory, 41
Vault services, 75

Wells Fargo Bank case, 84, 85,
  99, 100, 101
Workpapers, uses of, 139, 140

Zero balance accounts, 48, 49